# JAGUAR WOMAN

## MELANIE WATT

KEY PORTER BOOKS

*To the people of Belize, who recognize the
immense wealth of their wildlands*

Canadian Cataloguing in Publication Data

Watt, Melanie
  Jaguar woman

ISBN 1-55013-149-4

1. Watt, Melanie.   2. Jaguars.   3. Photography of
animals – Belize.   I. Title.

QL31.W38A3 1989   599.74′428′0924   C89-094077-0

Typesetting: Southam Business Information and
Communications Group Inc.
Printed and bound in Canada by
T. H. Best Printing Company Limited

Editor: Sarah Swartz, The Editorial Centre
Design: Denise Maxwell

Key Porter Books Limited
70 The Esplanade
Toronto, Ontario
Canada   M5E 1R2

89  90  91  92  93   5  4  3  2  1

# CONTENTS

Acknowledgments

Foreword

1　The Spirit of the Jaguar　1

2　Preparing for the Cross-Country Classic　15

3　Riding for the Jaguar　27

4　Tales and Warnings in the Bush　43

5　Life in the Bush　71

6　Tracking the Jaguar　97

7　Bringing in the Jaguar　121

8　The Future of the Jaguar　143

# Acknowledgments

World Wildlife Fund Canada provided both financial and moral support. Thanks especially to Steven Price. Jaguar Canada Inc. provided funding for the jaguar reserve, and so helped ensure its future. I am grateful not only for their support but also for John Mackie's genuine concern about the company's namesake. I also appreciated the support of the Belize Audubon Society, the Belize Ministry of Natural Resources, and the Belize Forestry Department.

The sponsors of the bike race are too numerous to mention, but I am grateful to them all, especially TACA airlines and the Fort George Hotel in Belize City. I am also grateful to Turhan Solis, Adrian Faux, Errol Gardiner and James Arana for their help in preparing for the Cross-Country Classic.

The individuals who help me with my research in Belize include Conrad Vincent Smith, Richard Lavigne, Ignacio and Pedro Pop, Edward and Kurl Smith and Renee Rourda.

For reading the manuscript and reminding me of events I had forgotten to mention, thanks to James Kamstra, Elaine Cristens, Mike Hingert, Rob Tuckerman, Wenda Watt, Virginia McLaughlin, Valerie Watt and Mom and Dad. Special thanks go to Derrick MacFabe for reading it over and over and for all his support and encouragement.

Thanks also to my editor, Sarah Swartz, for her expertise combined with patience and understanding.

A special thank you to Mom and Dad for all their support and for not worrying too much (at least not in front of me).

# FOREWORD

Through her pursuit of scientific knowledge in the jungles of Belize and the laboratories of Toronto, Melanie Watt has become one of the world's most noted jaguar experts. But getting there was not easy. The following pages are filled with the fascinating story of the personal struggles and triumphs she encountered on the way.

I am the chief executive of Jaguar Canada Inc., and our company is part of Melanie's story or should I say Melanie is part of our story for she has certainly earned a place in our respected history as an automobile company.

As one of the best-known British companies in the world, Jaguar is constantly approached by a myriad of organizations and individuals interested in having us sponsor one event or another. But we are relatively small as car manufacturers go, and do not normally participate in big-ticket sponsorship campaigns.

One day near the end of winter, 1985, a determined 22-year-old biologist helped show us a new way. From the moment Melanie Watt walked into my office at Jaguar Canada headquarters in Bramalea, Ontario, her enthusiasm proved instantly contagious.

She informed us that the corporate mascot – which our founder Sir William Lyons adopted as a model name in 1935 – was in trouble. If nothing was done by the year 2000, she insisted, the cat's demise as a species might be irreversible. This was unacceptable to me and to our Chairman and Chief Executive, Sir John Egan, and in fact to the more than 12,000 Jaguar employees worldwide. We all shared the view that the jaguar had been very good to us over the years and here was an opportunity to begin repaying the favour.

Several months later, we rallied our parent company in the United Kingdom and our associate company in the United States to join Jaguar Canada in a three-year, $100,000 commitment to Project Jaguar, our most important sponsorship campaign ever.

Today, nearing the end of the first instalment, the results have been nothing short of incredible. The Cockscomb Basin Jaguar Preserve in

Belize is now an accessible, fully operational wildlife sanctuary with three full-time wardens and a park director.

Poaching and habitat depletion have diminished and visitation is overflowing. At times the guest houses and wilderness trails are filled to capacity with people from as far away as Poland, Italy, Australia and Japan; HRH The Prince of Wales's name appears prominently in the guest register!

But what is more important are reports of more jaguar sightings. From ground scrapes and footprints to the actual *Panthera onca* itself, jaguars are coming back to the Cockscomb. As John Arnone, our public relations manager, said after returning from a recent trip to the Preserve, "There are new heartbeats in the rain forest."

Project Jaguar is our commitment not only to jaguar preservation, but also to the safety of thousands of animal and plant species that live and grow together in the rain forest. Thanks to a nudge from Melanie Watt, we now count ourselves as part of a growing community of corporations working towards the betterment of the environment.

John Mackie
President, Jaguar Canada, Inc.
Toronto, July 1989

# 1

# THE SPIRIT OF THE JAGUAR

It was now more than two months since I had arrived in Belize to live in the tropical forest and study the jaguar and, still, I had not had even a glimpse of one of these elusive spotted cats. I had known it wouldn't be easy to find a jaguar in the wild, but I was starting to wonder if I would ever see more than the tracks the cat left behind.

My friend Renee, here from Toronto on a two-week visit, would be leaving the next morning. If we couldn't see a jaguar in the flesh, I had hoped we would at least be able to get a photograph of one by using a pressure-plate system for my cameras and some catnip as bait. We picked a small cleared area at the edge of the dense bush off to the side of an old dirt logging road, which seemed a likely place. The idea was that, if a jaguar appeared at this spot to smell the catnip, it would step on the board and the cameras would go off, giving us the photograph we were looking for. It was awkward and time-consuming to set up the rain protection for the equipment, so time had quickly passed and it was now almost dark.

I opened the bag of catnip and dumped a handful onto the wooden plank. When I touched the board, the camera flashed in response. The trip mechanism was ready to "catch" a photograph of a jaguar. It was too dark now to try to set up the third camera, so I put it back into the Rover, and went back to check the two cameras one last time. Suddenly I heard a crash in the jungle behind me. "There's a jaguar back there!" I yelled as I dove into the Land Rover and hit the window shut. Renee stood outside, looking amused. "What makes you think it was a jaguar? We hear noises all the time. Anyway, you told me that jaguars don't hunt people." I slowly got out of the Rover and walked back to the camera set-up. I dumped the rest of the catnip and hurried back to the vehicle. "I don't know why, but I know it was a jaguar. And you're not the one with catnip all over your hands!" We laughed as I started up the engine and headed slowly forward around the bend in the road.

"Look!" I yelled as my headlights flashed onto something moving on the road ahead. A beautiful spotted cat was walking away from us, down the road. It stopped and turned, and even though I was in the car, my heart skipped a beat. I had waited a long time for this. I could see powerful muscles under its thick coat. It stared at us for a moment and then turned and walked away, down the middle of the road.

I followed at a distance, and it paid no attention to the rattling Land Rover moving steadily behind it. It was obviously not interested in us. As I moved closer, it stepped off the road and looked back, as if waiting to be passed. When I didn't proceed, it resumed the centre of the dirt road and continued on. I noticed a complete lack of fear in the jaguar's eyes, and it was unnerving. I reached the camera out the window and, when the flash went off, the big cat leapt into the bushes in one bound and was gone.

I had finally seen my first jaguar. Renee couldn't believe her luck at seeing one on her last night in the Cockscomb. We stared into the darkness, but the jaguar did not reappear that night.

When I heard about the possibility of going to Belize, my first reaction was "Belize? Where is it?" I have heard this question enough times now that I immediately explain that Belize was once called British Honduras and is just south of Mexico's Yucatan peninsula. As a zoology student, I was especially interested in Belize because of its tropical forests and extensive wildlife.

As part of an undergraduate course in zoology, I had been studying land hermit crabs in the laboratory. I was planning to spend several weeks studying the same behaviours in the field, to see if hermit crabs behaved the same way in the wild. I had saved up enough money from my part-time job at a bicycle store to pay for my airfare to the tropics. For several weeks I asked all the members of the zoology department if they had been anywhere where they'd noticed an abundance of hermit crabs. One student, Joe, had been studying tapirs in Belize and said he had seen hermit crabs there, but that it would likely be too difficult to set up a study area there in such a short period of time. I ended up spending several weeks at Huntsman Marine Laboratory in Barbados for my field-work.

Two months after I returned to Toronto, and just a few weeks before starting graduate school, Renee and I were in our laboratory when Joe knocked on the door. He had just found out he was going to Belize again and, if I wanted to go too, he could point me in the right direction once we got there. I thanked him, but explained that I had already done my field-work. He said to think about it anyway because it would be a great chance to see the tropical forest, and since there was a seat sale, the flight wouldn't cost too much. After he left, Renee turned to me and said, "Are you crazy? You just had a chance to actually see the tropics and its wildlife and you turned it down!"

Even after I explained that I had barely enough money to cover the flight and that I would miss several Saturdays at the bike shop and lose even more money, Renee was not impressed. She kept telling me that it would be worth it and that I probably wouldn't get to go anywhere for years, now that I had decided to go to graduate school.

I was just starting to find her argument convincing when Joe came back with a stack of books on the tropics. I flipped open one book and a beautiful toucan stared back at me. "You don't actually see these flying around there, do you?" I asked. Joe said toucans were fairly common in Belize and I might even get lucky and see a scarlet macaw. That did it! I had done a project on captive macaws for one of my undergraduate courses. Since they are so rare, I had never dreamed I might actually see one in the wild.

Joe said there were several scientists studying jaguars and other wild cats in southern Belize and that I might be able to visit the area that was soon to become a jaguar reserve. I had seen wild cats only in the zoo, and this prospect sounded exciting. "Okay, I'll go !" I said excitedly before my more practical side had a chance to object. I had to get my shots, take malaria pills and pack my bags. And then, before I knew it, I was on a plane to Central America.

When I first arrived in Belize, in August 1984, I took a bus to Cayo, a town near the Guatemalan border. I was on my way to see Mayan ruins in Tikal, Guatemala. The bus picked up anyone who waved it down along the route. It was comfortable and not too crowded, but the music blaring through the loud speakers made sleeping impossible. Suddenly, without warning, the bus stopped and the driver told us to get off without our luggage. I had been warned about the dangers of going to Central America, and was now worried that I had dismissed them too lightly.

I got off the bus with everyone else, but I was having trouble understanding the Creole instructions. The bus then drove off down the highway without us! My suspicions were dispelled when someone explained to me, in language that I could understand, that the bridge was under construction and the driver was afraid it wouldn't hold the weight of the bus and all its passengers. We crossed the bridge on foot and got back into the bus on the other side. My fears for my safety in Belize turned out to be largely unfounded. Belize is a democratic country, and even the policemen don't carry guns.

From the air, Belize is very rugged-looking. Its mangrove-lined coast gives way to dense jungle inland. Belize's mainland is about 162 miles (280 km) from north to south and about 62 miles (109 km) from east to west, giving it a total of only about 9,200 square miles (22 000 km²). Unlike the surrounding countries, Belize has a rather low population density. There are more than 200,000 people in Belize, and 50,000 live in Belize City. Much of Belize is virtually uninhabited bush, because most of its people live in cities, towns or villages.

I have never been very good at learning other languages, so I was more than pleased to discover that Belize's official language is English. The local English–Creole dialect is almost impossible to understand on first hearing, but I eventually became quite adept at it. About 10 percent of the population are Mayan, while about 40 percent are Creole, 33 percent have Spanish ancestry and 7 percent are Garifuna. The Creole are those who have some degree of African ancestry and speak the local Creole dialect. The Garifuna originated from the island of St. Vincent, when the black Africans of the slave ships mixed with native Carib Indians. Most Belizeans are a mixture of several groups, and 86 percent speak English and the English Creole.

Sugar and citrus are Belize's biggest exports, and rice, maize, bananas and beans are also important crops. When Belize was first colonized and developed, logwood and mahogany were greatly exploited. Now forestry exports comprise only about 2 percent of foreign earnings.

It seemed to me that Belize's richest resource was its wildlife. Many animals that are rare in other countries are common here. Belize has many animals not often seen in other countries, such as brocket deer, tapir, howler monkeys, jaguarundis, margay, ocelot, cougar and, of course, the elusive jaguar.

Challenge and romance surround the image of the jaguar, perhaps because so little is known about its behaviour. In fact there have been very few scientific studies done on jaguars in the wild and these have produced variable results. While most other members of its genus have been studied, little research has been done on the jaguar, probably because of its preference for solitary and nocturnal activity in the dense jungle. Such solitary behaviour means that extensive tracking and travel through dense bush are required if several individual jaguars are to be monitored.

Because of their perceived threat to man, jaguars are often killed if they are found near settlements. Thus, remote and isolated areas are preferable for research, but these areas are more difficult to work in. In dense tropical bush, travel is slow until trails and roads can be carved out of the vegetation.

Much of the information available on the jaguar's distribution and abundance was gathered from data on the number of jaguars killed in various areas during the fur trade. The one book I could find about jaguars was based almost entirely on anecdotal evidence from tropical hunters. Even basic information about the jaguar varies dramatically. For example, the home range of individual jaguars has been reported to be as small as 1 square mile (2.5 km$^2$) and as large as 150 square miles (390 km$^2$). By the early 1980s it was obvious that more information was needed about the jaguar's habitat, eating habits and day-to-day behaviour.

At the time of my first visit to Belize, the New York Zoological Society (NYZS) and the Belize Audubon Society were working together to have an area of 145 square miles (360 km$^2$) called the Cockscomb Basin declared a jaguar reserve. Zoologist Alan Rabinowitz of NYZS was just completing a study on jaguars in the Cockscomb. He had originally gone to Belize when the Belize Audubon Society requested that NYZS send someone to assess jaguar abundance and locate an area in Belize to set aside as a reserve for jaguars. After a short tracking survey, Rabinowitz recommended the Cockscomb Basin, based on the survey as well as on such factors as land ownership and future development potential. Rabinowitz then concentrated his studies of jaguars in the Cockscomb Basin.

The Belize Audubon Society and NYZS worked together to establish the Cockscomb Basin as the first area in the world set aside specifically to protect jaguars. The Cockscomb, at the base of the country's highest peaks, was a great place for a reserve because it was surrounded by mountainous jungle areas that made travel difficult for even the most enthusiastic poacher. There was only one passable road into the basin and it could be monitored. A gate and signs could be placed at the Mayan Indian village at the road entrance from the Southern Highway.

There were other reasons for protecting the basin. The steep slopes in the Cockscomb would be susceptible to erosion if the vegetation were to be removed. As well, since two large rivers originate in the basin, maintaining the vegetation density was vital to prevent flooding of the Southern Highway in the rainy season, which would put the water supply to the towns and villages in the area at risk. Protecting the wildlife and its habitat in the Cockscomb meant that surrounding villages would also be protected.

On that first trip to Belize, I went to see the Cockscomb Basin, home of the future jaguar reserve. I was immediately enchanted by the area. I had never been in a tropical forest before, and the jungle in the Cockscomb is particularly dense because it has been logged, which promotes lush secondary growth. The trails into the bush had been hand cut with machetes and were just wide enough for one person to pass without being pulled at by the surrounding vines, many of which were covered with thorns. The jungle was teeming with life. Beautiful, exotic-looking humming-birds were especially common and made their presence known by the noise of their wings as they hovered over flowers. Toucans flew overhead, and huge brilliantly coloured butterflies fluttered along the trails in front of me. As I approached, lizards would zip off rocks where they had been basking in the sun. Jaguar tracks could often be found along the roadway and trails.

Though I didn't see any jaguars during this first visit, I became interested in their plight when I learned that these powerful cats were faced with extinction. I whole-heartedly supported the idea of the preserve and hoped it would come to fruition. Little did I know at the time that not only would the reserve be established, but it would become my home and the jaguar the object of my interest and work.

The very fact that jaguars are so elusive was what first piqued my interest in them. Though I had been fascinated with animals since childhood, I realized that, of all the big cats, I knew the least about the jaguar. My journey to the Cockscomb Basin left me wanting to know more.

Jaguars are the biggest cats in the Americas, even bigger than the cougar (mountain lion), with which I was more familiar from my camping experiences in western Canada. Jaguars live only on the American continent, in many different types of habitat, but usually in areas that have a lot of plant cover, a good water supply and sufficient prey. They belong to the genus *Panthera*, which also includes lions, tigers and leopards, but not cougars.

Jaguars are smaller than lions and tigers, but slightly larger than leopards. At a glance, jaguars can be mistaken for leopards, because of the similarity of their spotted coats. Both species have rosettes on their flanks, but within the jaguar's rosettes there are often one or more small black spots. The leopard's coat is usually missing these small spots, but, even so, it is not always possible to tell whether a pelt is from a jaguar or a leopard. The jaguar is a heavier, more compact and more powerfully built cat than the leopard, and its head is more robust, although its tail is shorter.

Jaguars are muscular cats with relatively short, massive limbs and a deep-chested body. They can weigh up to 350 pounds (158 kg), but in Belize they tend to be smaller. Six males that were captured and weighed in Belize had an average weight of only about 125 pounds (57 kg). That is still a lot of cat! Female jaguars are usually about 10 to 20 percent smaller than males.

Most jaguars have a yellowish coat with black spots, but some look solid black. If a black jaguar stands in the sunlight it is usually possible to see the faint dark rosettes and spots on its coat, and in fact the dark and spotted varieties belong to the same species, and young with both types of colouring can be found in the same litter. Albino jaguars have been reported in the wild, but they are rare. In some parts of the jaguar's range, dark animals are more common than spotted ones; however, in Belize, spotted jaguars are most common.

Almost all the information collected about reproduction in jaguars has been discovered from studying captive animals. There are usually two cubs per litter. After a gestation period of about 100 days, the young are born with their eyes shut and don't open them until they are about eight days old. The cubs may be born in a cave, under an uprooted tree or in an otherwise sheltered area. They have long, woolly, spotted fur with black stripes on their faces.

When they are born, the cubs usually weigh about 28 ounces (800 g), and gain about 2 ounces (48 g) per day for the first two months. They don't walk until they are about 18 days old and they begin to follow their mother at about six weeks of age. They may start eating meat as early as ten weeks after birth, but they continue to suckle for up to six months.

Young jaguars may be killed by crocodiles and by large snakes. A female jaguar will not allow a male near her cubs, because male jaguars, like male tigers, sometimes eat their own young. The cubs may stay with the mother for up to two years, and sometimes young pairs of cubs travel together. Otherwise jaguars are usually solitary animals.

Males and females meet only briefly for mating. During mating periods the adults make a vocalization that sounds like a hoarse, barking cough, repeated several times. These calls may be used to locate and/or to determine the reproductive condition of the respond-ing jaguar. Female jaguars reach sexual maturity when they are two to three years old; the males, when they are about three to four years old. Most jaguars don't reproduce after they are about eight years old. Captive jaguars have lived as long as 22 years, but in the wild most jaguars don't live past 11 years of age.

Jaguars are very skilled hunters. They kill their prey by stalking or ambush. In fact, the word "jaguar" is thought to have originated from one of the Tupi-Guarani languages and means "wild beast that overcomes its prey at a bound." Unlike some cats, jaguars seem to enjoy the water, and have even been seen swimming between islands.

There are reports of jaguars using their tails to attract fish to the surface of the water before scooping them onto shore. I think it is more likely that their tails just happened to flick the surface of the water as they were watching the fish. Because of their powerful, stocky build, jaguars are not the most graceful of cats, but they are quite adept at climbing trees.

Jaguars usually kill their prey by biting through the nape of the neck. But for larger prey, such as cows, they jump on the animal's back and use one paw to pull the head around, putting the prey off balance. The prey's neck is usually broken in the fall. Unlike tigers, jaguars rarely bite the throat to kill their prey, nor do they asphyxiate their prey as leopards do.

One of the most grisly but fascinating stories about jaguars is how they kill capybaras. Capybaras are the world's largest rodents; they can grow to be up to 4 feet (120 cm) long, can weigh more than 110 pounds (50 kg) and resemble overgrown guinea pigs. Jaguars frequently prey on young capybaras, biting at right angles to the head, and sometimes inserting their canines in the ear of the victim before cracking the capybara's skull like a nutshell. There are no capybaras in Belize, and even though I knew that jaguars didn't include humans in their list of prey, this vivid description of their killing technique didn't exactly make me feel confident about tracking them through the bush on my own.

Smaller prey are often killed with a single hit with the paw on the head. Once the prey is dead, the jaguar will sometimes drag it quite a distance. Even large prey is moved in this manner. Jaguars have been reported to drag their prey more than 1¼ miles (2 km), and have even been seen crossing rivers with large prey in their mouths. Jaguars tend to avoid eating the prey's intestines, and have even been known to remove them carefully from the carcass and deposit them some distance away. If they are disturbed while feeding, jaguars may return to the kill within a few hours or up to three days later. Unlike tigers and cougars, jaguars don't seem to try to hide their kill.

Jaguars have been reported as eating everything from avocados to anacondas. More than 80 different prey species have been documented, including monkeys, kinkajous, sloths, porcupines and iguanas. Jaguars are commonly thought to be nocturnal, yet many of their prey species are diurnal. Their favourite foods include peccary, capybara, armadillo, paca, agouti, caiman and turtle. Reports have been filed of jaguars flipping huge sea turtles on their backs before scooping out the insides.

The jaguar's range once extended from the southwestern United States, in Arizona, New Mexico and Texas, but the animal had disappeared from that area by the early twentieth century and has since also disappeared from El Salvador, Uruguay and the developed areas along the Brazilian coast. Its range is now limited in Argentina, Guatemala and Mexico, and it is endangered in Bolivia, Panama, Costa Rica and Honduras. Jaguars are also considered rare in much of Colombia, Peru and Venezuela.

Fossil remains of jaguars have been found as far north as Washington, Nebraska and Maryland. In more recent history, jaguars were found from the southwestern United States to southern Argentina and were important to the Mesoamerican Indian cultures. Though much of the history of the Mesoamerican Indians has been lost, evidence of the jaguar lives on in much of their art.

For the Mayans, animals were symbolic, and the jaguar and the eagle most often represented the Mayan rulers or head chiefs. "Balam" is the general Mayan term for jaguar, but the word can also mean priest. In the Mayan religion, the god who rules the world and its interior is portrayed as a jaguar. The sun god, Kinich Ahau, also has jaguar features. Jaguars were associated with sorcery and curing powers as well as with the underworld. During solar eclipses, it was believed that the sun was devoured by the jaguar.

In the Aztec culture, the jaguar stood for the earth and the underworld. The eagle served the god of the daytime sky and sun, whereas the jaguar attended the god of the nocturnal sky and the nocturnal sun of the underworld. A rain god and a fertility god were also represented by jaguars. The Aztec military included the order of the eagle and the order of the jaguar. Only warriors of merit were admitted to these orders, which were in ceremonial opposition to each other. The Aztec god of the royal cult was known as Tezcatlipoca and was thought of as a jaguar.

Though the jaguar played an important role in these Indian cultures, it seems to have been even more prominent in the Olmec culture. Olmec art focused on jaguars, and were-jaguars (combinations of jaguars and men) were extremely common. The jaguar was often a "nahual," which is an animal associated with a certain man so closely that the man's life depends on that of the animal. For the Olmec, the jaguar was both the totem and the nahual of the supreme leader. From 1500 to 1200 B.C., the Olmec formed a jaguar cult, which was later adopted by the Zapotecs and the Mayans and was preserved up to the Aztec period. For these cultures the jaguar symbolized terror and the mystery of the jungle and the underworld. It also represented strength, bravery and nobility.

Since the decline of the Native Indian cultures in South and Central America, the jaguar has been seen not as a deity, but as a source of wealth for the hunter. In 1968 alone, more than 13,000 jaguar skins were exported to the United States.

Hunters became quite effective predators and used dogs especially trained to track jaguars through the bush and to tree them for the hunters to shoot.

Methods for killing jaguars have been outlined in various old hunting books. There, it is explained that the most common and least expensive method is to follow vultures to a fresh kill and then wait until the jaguar comes back to feed. Many hunters also try to mimic the jaguar's call, using a variety of instruments: some grunt into a hollow gourd; some tug on a waxed horsehair cord within a hollow gourd; others use a short wooden trumpet or a conch. One author suggests using a half-filled teapot as a jaguar caller. Another method mentioned in the hunting guides, specifically for ridding oneself of livestock-killing jaguars, is to put out a poisoned carcass or set up a shotgun trap.

By the end of the 1960s, public awareness of environmental issues and of the need for conservation of endangered species was just beginning. This awareness soon had an impact on the fur trade. The number of jaguars had been drastically reduced through fur-trade hunting, and larger expenditures of time and money by hunters to find the diminishing number of jaguars caused the price of jaguar furs to rise and drew public attention to the problem.

The mass slaughter of these majestic cats for their fur was slowed dramatically in 1973, when the Convention of International Trade in Endangered Species of Wild Fauna and Flora (CITES) listed the jaguar in Appendix 1, thereby providing the cat with its highest level of protection. Now, in every country where CITES is in effect there are strict regulations involved in the trade of jaguars or their products, and trading for commercial purposes is banned. Unfortunately, not all parts of the jaguar's range are under CITIES guide-lines – Mexico, for example – and even though jaguars are legally protected, these laws are not always enforced. Though there are many laws and stiff penalties for trade in skins throughout the jaguar's range, there is still a black market, largely spurred on by North Americans and Europeans who want the fur at any cost.

The full impact of the fur trade on the jaguar has never been determined. Jaguars are extremely difficult to census and therefore no information was available on their population or abundance before the fur trade. What was known was that jaguars were much less common after the massive killing spree.

The jaguar has been threatened on two fronts, not only through direct hunting but also through massive habitat loss. Jaguars are rarely found in areas of dense settlement. Because of the expanding human population throughout Latin America, the jaguar's range was rapidly shrinking as forested areas between large human settlements became smaller and more isolated. The largest remaining population of jaguars occurs in the Amazon rain forest in Brazil, but because of the huge variability reported in jaguar home-range size it is impossible to estimate the numbers of cats that might be protected there or in other countries within its range.

The conservation laws were brought into effect, not because the jaguar population had fallen below a critical number of individuals, but rather because it was known that there was a dramatic decrease in numbers. It was estimated that jaguars might become extinct by the year 2000, but without more information it was, and still is, impossible to say if that is a pessimistic or optimistic prediction.

One factor that interferes with the conservation of the jaguar is the fear of its potential threat to the lives of people and their livestock. In fact, however, though jaguars obviously have the power to overcome a person, they rarely attack people. While stories of other big cats attacking humans abound, there are few, if any, verified reports of jaguars becoming man-eaters. There does not seem to be a good explanation for why jaguars don't kill people, but this trait makes them more attractive for conservation than, say, the tiger, which is not so discriminating in its tastes.

Hunters often reported being "stalked" by the "ferocious" cats, and gave self-defence as an excuse to kill the jaguar. Jaguars do tend to follow people in the bush, but it seems to be more out of curiosity than anything else. Unarmed people have been followed by them, but not attacked. I was told by a Mayan Indian woman that she had found her children playing in a small clearing, with a jaguar lounging on a tree branch above them. She had gathered her children immediately and taken them home, but the jaguar had not appeared interested in either her or the children.

I heard several stories, told by hunters, of jaguars walking through camp areas and stealing fresh meat and domestic animals. Individual jaguars have been known to develop a preference for certain livestock, such as cattle, pigs and horses. If that particular jaguar is removed, the livestock killing stops, even though other jaguars are still in the area.

Though the fur trade has taken its toll on the jaguar population, the biggest threat to this feline is now habitat loss. As the tropical forests of the world disappear, so does the jaguar. Most researchers agree that jaguars need a large habitat area to survive. This finding led to the establishment of the jaguar reserve in the Cockscomb Basin.

The Cockscomb Basin became the first reserve in the world set aside specifically for the jaguar, but it was not established to help a population of jaguars at the expense of everything else. In fact, one of the reasons that the jaguar is an important animal to protect is because it is among the most vulnerable. It is at the top of the food chain and would be one of the first species to disappear. An area that could support a healthy population of jaguars could also support many other indigenous species of plants and animals. It would have been extremely difficult to raise funds or gain publicity for a specific species of frog or mosquito that might occur in the Cockscomb, but they will now be protected as well.

# 2

# PREPARING FOR THE CROSS-COUNTRY CLASSIC

**B**efore I left Belize, I spent several days in Augustine, a small village in the western mountainous pine-forest area. I was sitting outside the general store, drinking some pop, when a group of young men came by, asking for volunteers to play soccer. I said "sure" and hopped off my stool before realizing from the look on their faces that they had had male players in mind. "Do you need players or not?" I asked matter-of-factly. They laughed, and after a bit more convincing I was on the field, waiting for the game to start.

It had been a few years since I had played soccer, and I had usually played in goal position, so I was very rusty on the field. But it was good to get some exercise again. After the game, we all went back to the store for a Coke. Everyone was telling me how well I played, which was embarrassing since I felt I had been sloppy. To redeem myself, I explained that I hadn't played soccer in a long time, and that my favourite sport was cycling. That comment was to change my life.

When they heard I was a cyclist, one of them said, "You should try to ride the Cross-Country Classic bicycle race. It's one of the biggest national events in Belize and no woman has ever finished it. The race starts in Belize City and goes across the country to the Guatemalan border, then turns around and comes back. It's been held every Easter weekend since 1929. In the old days, the cyclists had to swim across creeks and rivers with their bicycles on their backs. They used to sleep overnight in the town of San Ignacio, the half-way point. But today the road is better and they do the whole distance in one day." No one knew exactly how far it was, but I was told it was more than 100 miles (160 km).

"I think that's a bit too far for me," I said, "especially since it's so hot here. Anyway, it's at the beginning of April. It would be too hard to train all winter in the snow in Toronto and then try to ride in Belize at the hottest time of the year."

They all agreed, except for one man in his early twenties whose imagination had been stimulated. "That would be something to see," he said, "a woman finishing that race! The guys have so much trouble cycling in the sun and wind that a lot of them have to drop out. You know, the race gets a lot of attention and local businesses sponsor the best riders for the publicity. I bet you could get a sponsor to pay your way down here, even if you don't finish the race."

"It sounds tempting," I said, "but with the amount of time I would need to spend training, I could work instead and make enough money for several trips to Belize." With that, the conversation went back to the soccer game, and it wasn't until I was leaving that the same young man spoke about it again.

"At least think about it, okay? It would be something you'd be able to tell your grandchildren," he said, with a grin.

"From the sound of that race, I might not survive and then there wouldn't be any grandchildren," I said, and they all laughed as I walked away from the small group sitting in the shade of the thatched roof.

Months later, long after I returned to Toronto, I received a letter from the Cockscomb with the good news that the jaguar reserve was now officially established. The bad news was that hunters were still poaching on the reserve, and the Mayans were still practising slash-and-burn agriculture within the reserve boundaries. Publicity was desperately needed to let people know that this area was a reserve and that it was illegal to hunt and farm there. It was also important to educate people about the need to protect the jaguar before it was too late. The government notices in the paper did not seem to be having an effect. A large publicity campaign was needed, but very little funding was available for one.

When I heard about this dilemma and the need for publicity, the cycle race suddenly came to mind. I wrote a letter to the Cockscomb and suggested to Rabinowitz that I could ride in the Cross-Country Classic, using the publicity to raise public awareness of the plight of the jaguar. All I had to do was finish the race to set the women's record. It was a challenge I could no longer resist.

I had done some bike racing in Canada, but was never very fast. I did seem to be able to ride distances though. It wasn't until after I agreed to ride the race that I found out it was actually 144 miles (230 km) long and that much of the road was gravel. By then, it was too late to change my mind.

Five months after my first trip, I was headed back to Belize to sign up officially for the race and to get sponsors and moral support for my "ride for the jaguar." The NYZS had said they would pay for this scouting trip, and in return I was to spend the week meeting with the Belize Audubon Society, the Minister of Natural Resources of Belize and potential local sponsors. I had not had any luck getting sponsors long-distance, but decided that if I could get letters of support from the Audubon Society and the Minister of Natural Resources, I might have more success, especially if I approached people in person.

I arrived in Belize with a list of names from the NYZS of the people I was to contact in the government and in the Belize Audubon Society. My bicycle was one of the first pieces of luggage off the plane, but the rest of my luggage didn't make it. I booked into a hotel and tried to contact someone on my list, but had no luck. The hotel owner told me of a boy down the street who was training for the Cross-Country.

I was soon in a back alley in the dark, wondering if it was really safe to be doing this at night. A dog growled on a porch and then started to bark at me viciously. I stopped and waited for it to calm down. Suddenly the door opened and someone looked out at me. "I'm looking for someone who rides the Cross-Country Classic. I need to find out more about it. Do you know anyone?" The door slammed shut and I was alone again.

I was just trying to decide if I should move on or knock again when the door opened and a boy of about 16 came out. It was Turhan, the boy whom the hotel owner had told me about. When I told him I was going to ride the race, he tried to discourage me by describing how difficult it was. When that didn't work, he said he would meet me at my hotel at five o'clock on Sunday morning. He and his friends were going for a training ride then, and I could ride along. That was more than I had hoped for. I rushed back to the hotel to try to put together my bicycle without tools; they were in my missing suitcase.

The next afternoon my bike was assembled and I decided to go for a 20-mile (32-km) ride, just to make sure everything was working. I rode slowly along the Northern Highway toward the airport. It was good to be riding the bike off the wind trainer I had been using in Toronto. After 10 miles (16 km) I turned around to ride home and was enjoying the scenery and the weather. A member of the Belize Audubon society, whom I had met earlier that day, pulled his car over to see if I needed a lift back. He said I had better hurry back before dark. It was just barely dusk, and I was sure I could be home before it got too dark, so I continued on my way. I had forgotten how fast night falls in the tropics.

Soon it was pitch black; there were no lights on the road and it was cloudy, so the moon offered no help. I could only tell where the road was by looking up through the trees on either side of it. Real and imagined noises were coming from the bush, and even from the roadway in front of me. I remembered hearing stories of people being badly hurt on motorcycles at night when they hit armadillos that ran across the road in front of them. Finally, I made it back to Belize City. From then on, I made sure I got back before dusk.

The following day I visited the Belize Audubon Society, which ran the Cockscomb Basin reserve. They were very pleased that I would be riding the bike race and promoting the plight of the jaguar, and volunteered to help me get further support. I next went to see Dean Lindo, the Minister of Natural Resources. The reserve fell under the jurisdiction of his ministry, and written support from him would be very helpful.

I was impressed with how accessible the members of government were in Belize. A member of Belize Audubon and I made an appointment and were soon waiting on one of the benches in the hall outside Dean Lindo's office. Several other people were waiting and they all felt assured that they would be able to get in some time that day, even though some had not made appointments.

When we first told Dean Lindo that I was planning to ride the

Cross-Country Classic, he looked very surprised and said, "There's no doubt it will generate a lot of publicity, but do you know what you're getting yourself into? This is no race like you have in Canada. It's twice as long as your races back home. And the roads are full of gravel and dust. The heat is unbearable. Every year we have riders from the United States or Britain who try and ride it, but they usually have to drop out because of the heat and the bad roads."

I told him I had talked to some of the other cyclists and that I thought I could finish the race if I concentrated on the distance and didn't worry about the speed.

Dean Lindo shrugged his shoulders and smiled. "At least they can't say I didn't warn you. Even if you don't finish, you'll still get lots of publicity for the reserve. I'll write you a letter of support that might help you get sponsors." As we rose to leave I thanked him and he shook my hand and said, "Good luck on that ride. You're going to need it."

A member of the Audubon Society came with me to some of the more prominent businesses in Belize and explained to them what I was trying to do. It was a good advertising opportunity since any business that donated money to the reserve would get a sign on my service truck during the race, as well as a mention in several press releases. It was also for a worthy cause: all the money was to go directly to the reserve.

Local support for the reserve was important, and we were worried it might be difficult to get the first sponsors. But two businesses in Belize City offered their support immediately and set the precedent. The first was the Fort George Hotel. Paul Hunt, the manager, offered me free accommodation for the two weeks leading up to the race. He suggested we go to see John Searle, the manager of TACA Airlines, one of the main carriers serving Central America. Paul and I went in to John Searle's office, where I was introduced to him as "the woman who was trying to protect the jaguars by riding the Cross-Country Classic." John Searle laughed and then asked who I really was. Paul and I explained in more detail, but Searle didn't look as though he really believed it. "Do you know what that race is like? There are bicycles and motorcycles and trucks weaving in between each other. It's hot, really hot, not like you're used to at home," he warned.

I was starting to get a little uneasy about the race with everyone telling me how impossible it was, but I pretended confidence: "I know all about the race and I think if I ride it we can gain a lot of publicity and raise some funds to keep the reserve operating."

"If you're crazy enough to ride that race, then I'm crazy enough to sponsor you with your airfare. I wouldn't want to be in your shoes on Easter weekend though," John Searle said, as he walked us to the door.

Once I received my first two pledges, getting others was easy. I walked into almost every business in Belize City and asked them to sponsor me in the race. Most people thought it would be impossible for me to finish, but agreed that my riding the race would generate a lot of publicity. Everyone was also pleased the money would be staying in the country. Almost every business I approached donated what they could. My week in Belize had really got things rolling. I now had local sponsors and letters of support from various local organizations.

Belize is not a wealthy country and I knew that it would be impossible to get enough money from local sponsors to set the reserve up and keep it going. It was also important to bring in an outside sponsor that would be in a financial position to supply the needed funds. When I had first decided to ride the race I had one obvious sponsor in mind: Jaguar cars. I told Paul Hunt about my plan and he suggested I write to Sir William Lyons, founder of the car company. Paul knew Sir William Lyons because they had both grown up in the same town in England. I couldn't believe my luck! Paul said he would write a covering letter, while I ran down to the Belize Library and found a ten-year-old *Who's Who* in which to look up his address. I took the letters to the post office and sent them special delivery. But it wasn't fast enough. I opened a newspaper five days later and found Sir William Lyons's obituary.

Once I was back in Toronto, I decided to talk to the Canadian office of Jaguar cars. I thought it might look a bit odd if I phoned up without a formal introduction, so I called World Wildlife Fund (Canada). I told them that I planned to approach Jaguar cars for a donation to the reserve and asked them if they could offer some support and advice. I was introduced to Steven Price, the vice-president of World Wildlife Fund (Canada). He was really interested in the project and said he would go to see the Jaguar car company with me.

Within a few days, Steven Price and I were on our way to see John Mackie, president of Jaguar Canada Inc. We explained the plight of the car's namesake and told him of the efforts being made to protect it in Belize. We were all set to explain how the sponsorship could develop publicity and benefit the car company, but we never got that far. As soon as John Mackie heard about the problems facing the jaguar, he suggested we ask for a sponsorship from all three branches of the car company, and he offered to discuss the possibility with the British and American offices.

The bike race was only a few weeks away and he couldn't guarantee a commitment by then. But his enthusiasm was more than we had hoped for in an initial meeting. Steven Price and I were hopeful it would go through. Steven suggested that WWF (Canada) could take care of the expenses for the race.

Now all that was left for me to do was to keep training for the bicycle race. I knew the heat would be my biggest problem, so I kept my apartment at 80°F (26°C) and bundled up warmly when I went outside. February and March are bad cycling months in Toronto. I used an indoor wind trainer hooked up to my bicycle and had a heater turned up beside it whenever I trained.

The training was going fairly well until I pulled two muscles in my left leg. I went to a doctor to get it checked and was told it was a common problem, but I would need to have my knee operated on. The doctor said there was no way I could ride the race. I couldn't believe it at first. All I knew was that I was committed to ride that race. I tried to convince the doctor that I could ride, then have the knee operation, but he insisted I shouldn't cycle.

Finally, in desperation, I went for a second opinion, and it was much more encouraging. If I followed a strict exercise schedule and used ice-packs, I might be able to ride the race. This was just what I wanted to hear. I did all I was supposed to do and felt reasonably strong by the time I was ready to go to Belize.

I thought I was prepared when I arrived in Belize two weeks before the race, but when I got off the plane, I felt like I had walked into a sauna. It was difficult to walk quickly and it was hard to imagine cycling in that heat. I headed out on a training ride with Errol, a friend of Turhan's, who was also training for the Cross-Country. It was extremely hot, but I was careful to drink lots of water. After about 20 miles (32 km) we both started to feel ill. We headed slowly back to Belize.

Suddenly I realized I couldn't keep riding. I got off the bike and lay down. Errol cycled back to where I was resting and tried to get me to move. It was then I realized I had just lain down where I was – in the middle of the Western Highway. Errol convinced me to get back on the bike and coast to a tree, where at least we could get into the shade. I felt just awful and he told me to drink some water. I drank both my bottles of water and then realized what I had done. We were still 15 miles (24 km) from Belize City and I had no water left. We knew we needed a ride.

I heard a vehicle coming and dragged my bike into the middle of the road and stood there. Errol was trying to get me to stand at the side, but I wanted to make sure the driver stopped. Fortunately, he did. The truck took us right into Belize City. When I got back to my room, I drank more water and fell asleep. Now I was scared. If I could feel like that after 30 miles (48 km), what would I feel like after riding almost five times that distance?

Though my training was not encouraging, the publicity I was generating couldn't have been better. Each of the country's papers carried at least one story about me in every edition. One day, an enterprising paperboy asked me if I wanted to buy a paper. When I said no, he said that if I didn't, everyone would know my race number before I did. So I bought the paper, and sure enough, on the front page was the headline "Melanie Will Wear No. 12 In Cross-Country Classic." People stopped me on the street to offer encouragement and I heard that betting was heavy as to whether I would have to "truck home."

One day I was alone on a training ride, with my head down, riding a flat stretch as fast as I could, when I heard a noise just off the edge of the road. I slowed down and turned around and peered into the scrub just past the shoulder of the road. Suddenly I heard a grunt and a squeal, and a peccary appeared from behind a bush in front of me. Peccaries are wild, pig-like mammals that have long bristly hair. Then I realized that there was a whole group of them within a few yards of where I was standing. They often travel in groups and grub for food with their snouts. They usually don't bother people, but they are unpredictable. I had heard that groups of them will kill dogs if provoked. I was standing a bit too close for comfort, so after watching them for a few minutes I continued on my ride. The wildlife in Belize never ceased to amaze me.

The Wednesday before the race was the annual meeting of the Belize Cycling Association. Everyone who would ride the race was to be there at 8:00 p.m. sharp. I had trouble finding the meeting-place. I got there at 8:10 and rushed into a room full of chatter and young Belizean males. I was so relieved to be there more or less on time, that I didn't notice the sudden hush that fell over the room. Eighty-five pairs of eyes were staring at me, and nobody said a word. Most of them had heard about me, but hadn't seen me before.

I was starting to feel uncomfortable, then Matthew, a cyclist I had met before, broke the silence by yelling across the room, "Melanie! Come sit over here!" As there were ten occupied seats on both sides of him, the suggestion provoked a murmur of chuckles. I said I was quite fine where I was, but he somehow managed to get the whole row to move over one and the guy on the end was bounced. Beaming, Matthew gestured gallantly and pulled out the now empty chair. So much for slipping into the meeting unnoticed.

When the laughter died down, the meeting started. By this time I knew a few of the participants, but I was a bit nervous about what the other cyclists would think about a foreign female, an outsider, riding their race. I was anxious about being accepted.

I had been on several training rides, and after the first few, everyone had relaxed and talked about the newest in bicycle gear. It helped that I worked in a bike shop at home and could tell them all about the latest equipment. Besides Turhan, Adrian, Matthew and Errol, I now recognized Lindy and Warren, two of the top cyclists in Belize. A few other faces looked familiar, but I couldn't remember many other names.

A few minutes after the meeting began, the president of the Belize Cycling Association announced to everyone that I was going to try to finish the race, although he thought it was highly unlikely that I could ride as far as San Ignacio. I told him I had already ridden that far. Chuckles again.

Understanding the local dialect was still a stumbling-block in my attempts to communicate with the cyclists. I was having trouble understanding people when they spoke in rapid Creole. Matthew rambled on for ten minutes about something, but I lost it in the first few sentences. He turned to me at the end of his speech and said, "Right, Melanie?" Luckily, Turhan and his friend Adrian were nodding in agreement, so I said "Right." I still don't know what I agreed with.

It was obvious that this was an important race. Each of us was handed a list of station prizes that would be given out to the first rider to pass by certain points along the race route. Most of the prizes were offered by small villages and by individuals along the route. Prizes included cash, a bible, a sheep and a bull. The race winners would receive cash and free flights to the United States. Each cyclist was allowed one motorcycle and one truck for service in the race. After the meeting was over we all paid a small registration fee and picked up the flags for our vehicles.

The next morning I went for a short ride to make sure my bike didn't need adjustments. I rode a few miles up the highway and turned around to come home. A few minutes later a car pulled up beside me. It had tinted windows and I couldn't see who was inside. I thought it might be someone I knew from Belize City, so I slowed down a bit. The car swerved sideways and cut me off. I tried to stop, but I couldn't, because my feet were strapped in. I was going to fall, but I had to make sure I avoided the car's wheels. There was dense bush on my right and I was about to dive into it, still strapped to the bike, when the car sped away. I looked up and Turhan, Errol and Adrian were cycling toward me. They didn't recognize the car and I had noticed there were no plates on the back.

We never did figure out who was in that car or what they wanted. Maybe they had just been curious and hadn't realized that, since my feet were strapped in, I would fall if I had to stop. But it made me nervous and I was careful not to ride alone after that. Except for that one incident, training rides were usually fun. Often people in passing cars would yell encouragement out their windows and sometimes stop to help if one of the group had a flat tire.

All of the cyclists with whom I trained were really helpful and supportive. They gave me pointers about the bike race and, most important, they kept telling me that they thought I could do it. This was the beginning of a network of cycling friends who would become a very helpful support system to me during my future work in the bush.

Three days before the race I met James Arana, who offered to be part of my service crew during the race. He had been born and had grown up in Belize, but had moved to New York when he was in his early teens. After ten years he was back on a visit. When I found out that he taught self-defence in the Bronx, and had often had to deal with training injuries, I thought he could be helpful if I or anyone else pulled muscles or otherwise got hurt in the race. I had promised every Belizean sponsor a sign on the service truck, and it took hours with a stencil and markers to make more than 20 of them on cardboard. James spent the whole day helping me.

All I could do for the week before the race was try to rest. I was as ready as I could be, and I was starting to get nervous about the race. Mom and Dad phoned me the night before the race and told me to be careful of the sun. I assured them that, if I felt I couldn't finish, I would just stop where I was and rest. The main thing was for me not to return by truck. If I had to, I would sleep overnight in the back of my service truck and continue cycling the next morning.

I went back to my hotel room and checked my bikes over one more time. One bike would be used as a spare in case I got a flat tire, had mechanical problems or crashed the other bike. The crew could then pass me the other bike from the truck and, one hoped, as long as I wasn't hurt, I could keep riding without much interruption. I put ice on my bad leg, and it felt strong enough. Tomorrow night at this time, it would be over. Then I would know if I really could ride that far.

# 3

# RIDING FOR THE JAGUAR

After four hours of good sleep, I woke up at 3:00 a.m. just before my alarm went off. I ate an orange and some toast that the hotel kitchen had given me the night before. James soon arrived and the truck picked us and my equipment up and brought us to where the race would begin. It was only 3:30 a.m. and there was already a big crowd. This race was more impressive than I had thought. I gave James and the rest of the crew instructions one last time.

I cycled up to the start line. It seemed as if everyone was watching me, and I felt uncomfortable. I rode farther, past the crowd along the road as it turns through the cemetery. Once the race started, this section of road would be crowded, but for now it was off limits to all but the cyclists. Most of the cyclists were back in the crowd, so for now I was alone in the darkness. It was quiet and calming. In four years of cycling, I'd never felt more comfortable on a bicycle than I did during those few minutes. I felt like cycling. If I couldn't do it today, I never would.

I cycled back to the crowded, noisy start line. Everyone was either giving or getting last-minute instructions. The race was to start in a few minutes, so I lined up at the front. The race route was simple. We were to ride straight along the Western Highway until it ended in the town of San Ignacio 72 miles (115 km) away near the Guatemalan border, then turn around and ride back toward the Caribbean Sea, finishing the race in Belize City. I had been told the course would get more complicated near San Ignacio when the first of the 86 cyclists, 86 motorcyclists, and 86 trucks turned around and headed back. There would be chaotic traffic in both directions.

Suddenly, someone called to me out of the crowd, "Good luck, Jaguar Girl!" I realized that in my nervousness I had lost track of the real reason I was riding the race. If people I didn't know were calling me "Jaguar Girl," it meant that the publicity was working. The fact that my truck was covered with so many sponsors' signs meant that I had the support of people who understood there was a problem with the preservation of jaguars and other wildlife. I hoped that people would now be made more aware that there was a jaguar reserve in the Cockscomb Basin and that it was important to protect jaguars throughout the country.

I checked my tire pressure one last time and stared forward into the darkness. My arm was jostled by the rider beside me, and I looked up, startled. "The start is pretty scary, you know. Just ride straight and steady for the first bit." I thanked this friendly cyclist and commented on his apparent lack of panic. He assured me it was there and I felt slightly better, until he mentioned that if he dropped out at least the whole country wouldn't know. I laughed aloud, but inside I wasn't laughing.

I waited in the dark for the gun to go off. Eighty-five other cyclists were nervously snapping their brakes and checking their tire pressure. Hundreds of people were watching from the side of the road and several hundred more were behind us on motorcycles and in service pick-up trucks that would be following the race.

The mayor of Belize City came up to shake my hand. "We appreciate what you are doing for the jaguars. Good luck on your ride!" Then he leaned toward me in the dark and said quietly and much more seriously, "It is a difficult race, and a dangerous one. The sun is very hot on the way back. If you cannot finish, don't worry. It is good enough that you tried."

Then he was gone and I suddenly felt that I shouldn't be there, in the midst of all these cyclists who had trained so hard. I wasn't sure that I could ride that far. I had never ridden this distance. Distance was not the main problem though; the gravel and the heat were.

Maybe I just wouldn't be able to finish. I resigned myself to doing the best I could do.

I thought of the newspaper articles and radio interviews in which I had confidently stated that I would finish the race no matter what, that I wouldn't "truck home." Suddenly I felt alone and scared. I tried to get back that sense of calm I had felt earlier, but it was gone. The gun sounded and we surged forward. The time for thinking was over.

There was a forward surge of bodies and bicycles. People cheered and cameras flashed in what was still the dark. I got my feet in the toe clips all right and just started to relax when I hooked handlebars with the cyclist on my left. I certainly had never hooked handlebars with anyone before and I was caught off guard. Crashing is bad enough, but crashing in front of 80 riders who are accelerating as fast as they can was not a cheery thought. I heard a voice beside me say just to keep riding forward. Easy for him to say! All of a sudden we were separate again and I was riding faster than I had ever ridden before.

Somewhere in those first few miles, I pulled both muscles in my leg again. I didn't really feel any pain. The muscles just gave way when I tried to accelerate, and then my left leg was just along for the ride. I was afraid I wouldn't be able to ride, but my leg seemed to be numb. I didn't feel it until after the race, when I tried to walk.

I had never ridden in such a big pack of cyclists before and it was intimidating. But when any of my friends rode by, they would yell words of encouragement. I just tucked down and kept pedalling. Bicycles and breathing. Gears changing. Then we hit the gravel. Shouts of disappointment filled the dark, as the gravel punctured tire after tire. Please, please, not a puncture. At 110 pounds (49.5 kg) I had never had to worry about punctures at home, but on this road it was different.

Rider after rider went past me. I could keep up to them for a bit and then they would pull ahead. I was starting to lose the main pack when three riders came up from behind. One of them yelled, "Melanie! Catch on !" and I whipped in behind the last rider of the trio and pedalled as fast as I could. I stayed there for a few minutes until I could not get my legs to go any faster. I thought I was in my light gear at the front, and I reached down to put it on the big ring. It would not go! I looked down and saw that I was spinning my feet in my biggest gear. I looked ahead and saw that we were actually catching up to the main group. "I can't ride this fast," both my mind and body told me.

I was just trying to convince myself to hang on, when my service handed me a water bottle from the motorcycle. I mumbled "no" and kept pedalling, but I had told all the people servicing me to make sure I drank a bottle of water every 20 minutes, no matter what. Looking sideways at the motorcycler slowed me down a bit and I came out of the wind screen. The wind hit me like a wall and the pack left me as if I was standing still. We had passed quite a few riders even in the short time I was with the group.

From then on, I hooked on to whatever groups I could, and made good time to Belmopan, which is at the 49-mile (78-km) mark. I got there in about two hours. That was the easiest third of the race. It had been cool at the start and the sun had just been rising. The wind had been at our backs, but soon I would have to turn and face it.

The main pack had already gone by and I was on my own now. I saw a bicycle up ahead in the distance and thought if I could just catch up to it at least I could get a bit of wind block and some company. I forced my legs to go faster. I did not increase my gear because I didn't want my muscles to jam up. It took a long time, but finally I was within 100 yards (91 m) of the cyclist ahead. Unfortunately, I did not recognize the rider. Oh well, I thought, if we share pulling the front, we would both go faster. I pulled in behind him, and he did not notice me, but his service helpers did. They yelled at him that he couldn't even ride as fast as a girl. He got angry and sped up quite a bit, but I sped up too. I had worked hard to catch him and I wasn't going to let him get away.

He couldn't shake me, so his truck got in front of him and broke the wind for him. As a result, he rode much faster, almost touching the back of the truck and leaving me behind. One of the few rules of the race is that cyclists must keep their distance from any of the vehicles and from any cyclists that are not part of the race. It is too great an advantage, getting pulled along in the truck's wake, so it's illegal. When they got 100 yards (91 m) ahead, they stopped blocking wind for him. I then caught up again. By this time he was going so slow that I got impatient and went by him. His "support" crew was giving him such a hard time about being behind me that it was difficult to be angry. A few miles later, he did pass me, but he and his bike were now in the truck.

If I knew then that most of the other riders I caught up with would do the same thing, I would not have looked forward to the rest of the ride. It is at least twice as hard to ride alone, especially in this race with the sea wind in one's face all the way back to Belize City. I think that most of the cyclists dropped out of the race when I caught up with them not only because I was female, but also because I had stated several times that I was not a great cyclist, but rather a zoologist trying to prove that the jaguars were worth saving. They felt it was a put-down of their cycling abilities.

At some point, my mind started to get a bit fuzzy. I looked up through the mist and saw a huge group of men, women and children standing by the road. There was nothing near them, not a village or any buildings. I wondered where they had come from. They must have walked a long way to see the race. They were yelling and calling my name. "Come on, Jaguar Girl, you can do it!" I sped up and raced through that crowd. A young Creole man ran beside me and handed me a peeled orange. As I took a bite, everyone cheered. I felt a wave of warmth spread over me. It was hard to believe they were cheering so enthusiastically for me.

A young girl yelled, "See you on the way back!" and I knew I had to come back. I had to finish this race. These people would be waiting for me. The shouts of encouragement did far more for me than hours of rest would have done. It made me feel that I was among friends and that people were depending on me. Runners in every little village gave me oranges and coconut water.

A short way past the Belmopan cut-off, I started to feel bad again. The rolling hills were tiring me out and so were the gravel and the pot-holes. I did not know this part of the road well and I kept hitting the wrong spots. Two young Creole men on bicycles with upright handlebars who were not part of the race started riding beside me. One said he used to be a racer. They told me which side of the road to ride on and which sides of the bridges were safest for the bicycle. One guy stopped riding after a few miles, but the ex-racer kept up with me. I made sure he stayed behind or beside me. I did not want to be disqualified for following too closely.

Only 85 miles (136 km) to go – I was not inspired by the thought.

The road got worse and worse and I began to wonder if I could really finish this race. I was not even at the half-way mark! Discouragement set in again. Then I saw dust. A lot of dust. It was the first cyclists returning. It had been a little while since I had seen my last cyclist and it would be good to see how all my friends were doing. It was not until the pack was within a few hundred yards of me that I realized the problem: 40 riders and 40 trucks and 40 motorcycles were bearing down on me in a thick cloud of dust. Each driver was intent on watching his cyclist and his motorcycle. The first driver saw me and waved me out of the way. Hold it a minute here! I am in this race too, (I thought) and I am not moving over into the gravel for a service vehicle! I am good at playing "chicken" when I have to.

As each truck moved over a bit to let me by, the next driver would see me and move over too. Truck after truck, and I never had to move onto the deep gravel shoulder. I did almost hit a few bumpers, though. The dust was the worst part. Sometimes I just shut my eyes for a few seconds at a time, because there was so much dust I could barely see my front wheel. It was easier to play chicken with my eyes shut anyway. Adrian had been at the front, and I yelled for him to get behind someone. He laughed. I later found out that he had just won a station prize. As the service vehicles and riders went by, there were shouts of encouragement and clapping from them as they saw that I was still riding. Finally the main bunch went by and I could see again. A few more groups went by, but they were not going as fast nor were there as many riders. Then nothing.

I caught up to a few stragglers, who were still, like me, trying to get to the half-way point. But when they saw me they suddenly developed mysterious cramps and asked to be taken into their trucks. The road seemed very empty, the gravel seemed deeper and for the first time I noticed that my whole body had developed a dull ache. I was approaching San Ignacio, the half-way point, where the racers turned around and headed back to Belize City. More people were lining the road, and they made me forget my problems once again. I saw some faces I knew in the crowd and sped even faster over the San Ignacio bridge.

I had been told not to look down while crossing the bridge, because you can see right through it, and the river is fast and wide and a long way down. I had to slow down when I got to the far side of the bridge because I was not sure which direction I was supposed to take around the park. There was a big crowd there and everyone was yelling and shouting encouragement. A policeman saw my puzzled look and waved me to the right. I sped around the crowded little park and was back on the bridge within a minute. Homeward bound! I got almost to the end of the bridge before I looked down, out of curiosity I guess. I suddenly felt queasy and could not stop looking at the water below. I stopped pedalling and started to wobble. The water was churning and my head was spinning. Then I was over it.

At the end of the bridge was a small hill, and because I was going so slowly coming off the bridge, I had to stand up on the pedals and work to get up it. As I got near the hilltop, the crowd on both sides of the road was cheering me on and I felt good again. Then I heard a "bang" and almost came off the bike. When I had all my weight on the upper pedal, the chain had slipped and the pedal suddenly fell, leaving me off balance. I regained my balance, but not my composure. When I looked at the crowd right in front of me, they seemed as relieved as I felt. An older gentleman had even run over to catch me if I fell. A bit shaky, I slowed up and sat down on the bicycle seat for the rest of the climb.

This was where the crowds were largest, and it was hard to feel bad for long. My confidence returned and I flew through the crowd as fast as my legs would go – which, by this time, was not very fast.

Then, abruptly, the crowds ended and the gravel began again. The 23 miles (36 km) of road between Belmopan and Cayo is difficult, with a lot of gravel and pot-holes. It was hard to remember that it had been this bad on the way out and that I had made it one way already.

Thud! I hit a pot-hole dead on and something happened in my back. It felt like the kind of kink that you get in your neck, but it was half-way down my spine. The nice thing about kinks in necks is that usually if you do not move, you do not hurt. It was impossible to avoid moving my back in my current situation. My legs were moving up and down, and every time they did, it felt like someone was twisting a knife in my back. It hurt more when I went over pot-holes, so I started to try to weave my way between them.

I was gritting my teeth and trying not to yell, when I realized that nobody would notice if I did. The motorcycle was 30 feet (9 m) behind me and the truck was even farther back. It made me feel much better to yelp at the very bad bumps. Then a village! There was no way I could sit up and take food, so I just sped up and converted my grimace into a half-smile. I guess I looked like I was trying hard, because everyone cheered and gave lots of food to my service vehicles.

Once I was out of the village again, I started my yelps. They were not enough to keep my mind off the pain and I started to get very weary. I realized that in my attempt to miss pot-holes, I had been veering all over the road. I was weaving so much I felt like I was putting on more miles going back and forth than I was going forward. I started to slow down. I wasn't sure how much longer I could put up with this. Certainly not another few hours. I had thought I might get sunstroke or crash or just lose consciousness. It had not occurred to me that I could be stopped by a stupid kink in my back.

Things started to get hazy. I wished my bike would just fall apart and then I could get in the truck. I remembered hearing stories of guys who had given themselves flat tires or broken their own derailleurs just so they could quit races. I had always thought that sounded stupid. But right now I understood. My mind began to wander. Then I saw a gaping pot-hole just in front of me. I started to reach for my brakes but not in time. I yelled in anticipation of the pain. Then I realized my back didn't hurt so much. In fact, it didn't hurt at all! Whatever had jarred out, I had just knocked back in place. Now I had to make up for lost time.

The young ex-racer who had shown me the road on the way out started riding with me again and I was glad of the company. I asked him if he knew of any public washrooms. I had drunk about 12 bottles of water in the last few hours, so I figured it would be good to know locations. It was a good thing I asked because there was only one public building, a school, and it was just a mile away. That was it for the next 60 miles (95 km). I rode right into the schoolyard and the people there were thrilled I had decided to stop there.

Anyone who has ever ridden 90 miles (145 km) in one sitting knows it's hard to walk when you first get off the bike. It is almost impossible to do stairs, especially with your riding shoes on. I felt rather ill suddenly, so I figured I had better get upstairs to the washroom before I ruined my image with all these kids who were staring at me as though I were some kind of hero.

Downstairs looked like a picnic. My whole crew was busy eating watermelon, oranges and sandwiches and drinking orange juice and coconut water. I felt like a kid who had pulled in a good haul on Hallowe'en. I joined in for the watermelon, and James tried to massage my calves back to normal. It felt weird to sit down. I guess I stopped for a total of 20 minutes and by that time I had figured out that the sick feeling I had was probably directly linked to the distance I had pedalled and that it would probably not go away for a long time.

I was just getting ready to shove off on my bike again, when a little girl approached me with a scrunched-up dollar bill in her hand. She said shyly that it was for me, to "save the jaguars." Another girl gave me a handful of coins. After spending months figuring out how to carry as little weight as possible on my bike I stuffed all the coins in my jersey pocket and headed off to shouts of "Good luck!" and "We'll be listening on the radio to make sure you get there!"

It was hard to get back into the rhythm of cycling. I was also a bit concerned about the amount of water I had obviously used up. Twelve full bottles and most of that must have been sweated out. I didn't even feel hot! Five more miles (8 km) and a hill loomed in the distance. Funny, I'd never noticed a hill there before. It was more like a bump in the road. I was struggling up the initial incline when a guy ran over the top and said, "I've been waiting for you!" and pushed me over the top. It was one of the guys who had been showing me the road on the way to San Ignacio a few hours earlier. I was a bit wobbly and afraid he would push me too hard. I am still not sure if that push was legal, but I certainly did not ask for it. The moral support was even more of a boost than the physical help. That guy must have stood there for over an hour just to help me over that bump.

Meanwhile, the sun had gotten very hot, as it was almost noon. My service asked if I wanted water dumped on me and I said no. They said I looked hot, and it seemed easier to agree than to argue, so I said, "Okay, but I'm not hot." The motorcyclist pulled up beside me, slowed down to my pace and dumped a water-bottle over my head. The water hit me like ice and my skin sizzled. It was quite a shock. I told them next time not to use a bottle from the cooler. They hadn't.

That bottle had been sitting in the sun in the back of the truck. They gave me a funny look and said I'd get a bottle over my head every 20 minutes, whether I wanted it or not. Okay, maybe I had been a bit warm.

There were big crowds at Roaring Creek, but I was having trouble focusing. I looked up once and saw an old, heavy-set lady jumping up and down, yelling, "Come on, white girl! You show 'em!" She was grinning and when I grinned back, she clasped her hands over her head in a victory sign. Someone yelled, "You can do it," and I responded, "I sure can," and everyone cheered. I was starting to perk up! Every once in a while I would hear a radio from a roadside farmhouse saying, "The Canadian girl is still riding. Someone just phoned in to let us know she passed their house!"

With 30 miles (48 km) to go, my support truck ran out of water and the motorcycle disappeared down the road to get more. I looked back and my truck was also nowhere in sight. They had almost run out of gas and had stopped to find some. After eight hours with a truck and motorcycle roaring behind me, I felt very alone without them.

A boy in his late teens, wearing work boots and riding an old ten-speed, was behind me. He said he had never ridden this far before in his life, but he was going to try to ride to Belize City with me.

The wind picked up. There had already been a good wind, but now I had to stay tucked up, with my hands permanently on the bottom of the handlebars. Every time I sat up I would be hit with a gust of wind. I was tempted to ride behind the boy beside me, but he was not in the race, so that would be illegal. Only 23 miles (37 km) to go!

It didn't seem so long, but I was riding pretty slowly because of the wind. It was now midday, and it was very, very hot. The road looked as though it was made of white light. I was drinking bottle after bottle from the cooler now. I needed water dumped over me at least every ten minutes. It was amazing how fast I would dry off, with the help of the wind and the sun. It felt best when the water hit the back of my neck. That was where I was getting the most sun. My arms were dark red, a colour they had never been before and, I hoped, would never be again. I checked my legs. At least I matched. Out of curiosity, I peeled back the edge of my shorts to see what colour I used to be. I looked like an ad for why people should wear suntan lotion. My service asked if I wanted to put some lotion on now, but I said I was almost home. In fact, I still had at least two hours left to cycle.

The guy riding beside me was starting to feel the heat too. We were both riding silently, with our heads down because the sun was burning our eyes. He yelled and I looked up fast. Just in front of us, stretched across the road, was a snake that was at least 5 feet (1.5m) long! I barely had time to swerve and just missed its head. I was afraid it would strike, but I felt nothing on my leg as I rode by. The other guy hadn't been able to miss the snake, and he rode over its tail, yelling as he went. Then he announced that the snake had a tire mark on it. It was already dead.

After that short burst of adrenalin, I was even more tired than I had been before. It was 1:30 in the afternoon, and I had been riding for eight and a half hours. I suddenly realized I could get in within ten hours if I sped up just a bit. But as soon as I did, my legs felt peculiar. I got dizzy, and then I couldn't even make my legs pump as fast as they had before. The guy on the bicycle behind me asked if I was all right. I said I thought so, but I really didn't. My body felt strange, very heavy, as though my limbs weighed a ton. I was riding with a good part of my weight on my arms, since my legs couldn't take the pressure.

I saw the gravel then. It ran for 10 miles (16 km), on and off. After that it was just 5 miles (8 km) to Belize City. Almost home! But I still had that stretch of gravel ahead of me.

It was a lot harder after I hit the gravel. I tried to maintain the same speed, but that required a lot more effort. A motorcycle approached me from Belize City. The rider pulled up to me and said he had been sent to see if I was going to make it. I said, of course I was! He grinned and told me there was a bunch of people waiting at the stadium, just for me. Then he disappeared, back toward Belize City.

I sped up a little and was trying to hurry through the gravel when I felt a severe pain at the base of my thumb. I let go of the handlebar, like it was red hot, and that almost caused me to crash, because I was carrying a lot of my weight on my arms. My hand hurt quite a bit; I must have pinched a nerve. I couldn't touch anything, nor could I move it. I was having trouble riding through the gravel using one hand, so I rested the back of my injured right hand on the bars. It didn't work very well, but it was a bit of an improvement.

It was slow-going now, but I had stopped worrying about the time. My riding position was pretty awkward, but at least it wasn't boring: I had to concentrate very hard to keep from crashing. The vibration caused by the gravel was beginning to wear me out. All my muscles ached, and even my teeth were rattling. The pain in my hand eased a bit, and I could at least turn it the proper way around on the handlebars.

I saw another motorcycle approaching from Belize City, this one ridden by a policeman. He was to be my escort, believe it or not. They usually have a lead motorcycle ahead of the first rider into Belize City, but I certainly wasn't expecting an escort of my own. The gravel was almost behind me, and there were even some people on the road, cheering. I tried to speed up, but I just couldn't.

Through the graveyard and past the start line. Unfortunately, that wasn't the finish line. My whole body was humming now: I was going to make it! The policeman turned on his siren as we came into town, and people came running out of their houses, cheering and clapping. Alvin Card, the Cycling Association treasurer, came out of his house and grinned. "You did it!" he yelled. Not quite, I thought. Some kids were running beside me. I asked one of them how far it was to the stadium. I had been there once, but my memory was a bit hazy. They said it was over the bridge and around the corner. When I got over the bridge, I sped up, and the guy who had been riding with me said, "Take it easy!" It was good advice. I almost had to stop after that burst, and my heart was thumping so hard I could barely hear anything else.

I rode into the stadium grounds and headed around the horse track. People were standing in front of me and I just assumed they would move out of the way. I was within 4 feet (120 cm) of the crowd, when one of them saw I was not going to turn and said, "No! That way!" and pointed to my right. I was riding through thick sand, and I turned my handlebars 90 degrees to the right to make the turn and that stopped me for a moment. My feet were strapped in and I thought I would fall. To avoid doing so, I pushed my legs as hard as I could and took the corner. I got on to the paved inner track and sped up so I could "sprint" for the finish.

I had picked up a good amount of speed, when an official at the corner said, "Slow down, girl. You have three more laps to go!" No one had said anything about four laps. I had been told that you finished on the track in the stadium. My body went numb. I still had

1.5 miles (2.4 km) left to go! I slowed up a bit, but the whole crowd was cheering, so I pushed it. I figured the worst thing that could happen if I crashed would be that I would have to walk in.

Finally I was on my last lap. I sped up again, but not as much as the last time.

Then, finally, it was over, ten hours after it began. I turned the bike around and went back to the finish. I was too tired to be excited, but I was incredibly relieved that it was over. I could see some familiar faces in the crowd. Some of the cyclists had waited around for me to finish. I even remembered to unstrap my feet before I stopped.

The head official came over to me and asked me if I thought I could get off my bike. It seemed like a silly question until I tried it. I swung my leg back to lift it over the saddle, but my leg didn't make it. I tried again, then several people helped and luckily held me when I came off and stood wobbling on the ground. They all laughed and said this often happened to riders. It felt very strange standing up. I now knew the true meaning of rubber legs. They would hardly support me.

There were a lot of people around me and my bike. The official suggested we separate me from my bike in the crowd, since a group of kids was interested in my bike. It's a small one because I'm 5 feet 2 inches (157 cm), and they hadn't seen a bike that small before.

I was told my time was ten hours and six minutes. It was much better than I had expected. I would have been happy with anything under 12 hours. It was only three o'clock in the afternoon and sometimes stragglers come in after dark, but this year I was to be the last finisher. Everyone I passed had dropped out of the race. I had finished fiftieth, out of 86 starters.

I was lifted into the back of my pick-up truck and we went back to the hotel. I had expected congratulations when I went into the lobby, because the staff had become good friends with me in the three weeks that I had been there. No one said anything and barely responded to my "Hi" as I limped to my room. As I reached my door I heard one of the desk clerks quietly ask James what had happened. I turned and said I finished 30 minutes ago. They hadn't had a radio, and they had thought that because I was in so early I had taken a truck home!

Everyone gave me a hug, which was quite brave of them as I was covered with dried coconut water, orange juice, watermelon, dust and sweat. Then they all left so that I could sleep.

I felt exhausted, but as soon as I lay down, I knew I wouldn't be able to sleep. My legs, arms and neck were so badly burned, I could not touch them to the bed. I took a cold shower, but it didn't help. I telephoned Mom and Dad and they were really glad to hear I made it in one piece. Then I called up a few of the other cyclists and they came over to the hotel. We drank many glasses of lime and water and talked about the bike race. The bunch of us headed out to get hamburgers. People stopped me on the street and congratulated me and told me how much money they had won betting on me. I was even easier to spot now because of my strange sunburn from the long cycling shorts and elbow-length sleeves.

Warren, who came second in the race, was in our group and started kidding around. "If I'd known you could get so much attention for coming in fiftieth, I would have slowed down," he said. I replied, "If I'd known that second place got a free ticket to Miami, I would have sped up!" Warren's friend Lindy, who was also a really good cyclist, joined us later. When I asked him how he'd done, he said, "You may not believe this, but you beat me!" It turned out that he had been right at the front but had had to drop out because of severe muscle cramps. After we ate, someone suggested we go dancing, and I laughed. It turns out that it's a tradition for the cyclists to go out dancing after the Cross-Country. The marathon was not quite over.

The dance place was packed, and people I had never seen before came over and shook my hand and made me feel like a celebrity. Warren was also getting a lot of attention because he had done so well. I looked over at him and laughed because he looked like he was going to fall asleep in his chair. "I don't know if I can stay awake much longer. You must be tougher than I am," he said, with a grin. I said I was too afraid to fall asleep and lean against my sunburn. I went up to get us ice water and as I walked through the crowd my arm hit a man's arm. He jumped back and explained that my sunburn was so hot it had burned him. Then he recognized me. "You're the Jaguar Girl who just rode the Cross-Country! I just want you to know that every year I buy a jaguar skin for my hotel. This year the same hunter came to sell me one and I got angry with him. I told him that he must not understand why you were riding in the race and that he should be ashamed. I'm sorry I bought them before, but I didn't know it was a problem. I'll never buy a jaguar skin again!" Suddenly I felt it had all been worth it.

I realized that I was completely exhausted and went back to the hotel. My skin was still burning, so I filled the bathtub with cold water and climbed in and went to sleep. I woke up later feeling uncomfortable, but at least the burning feeling was gone.

Two days later, I was in Belize Airport, waiting for my flight home. I said goodbye to my friends and went to the immigration counter. The officer took my passport, stamped it, and was about to hand it back when he took it back. "I don't think we should give this back to you, miss." I was feeling really sad about leaving Belize and all the people I had met, and this was the last thing I needed – trouble with immigration.

"But, my passport's in order, isn't it?" I asked. He smiled at the officer beside him and showed her the passport. "If you don't have your passport, you won't have to go home!" He had heard me say during a radio interview that I didn't want to leave Belize. I laughed and reached for the passport but he tossed it to the next officer. We played a good-natured game, with me as the monkey in the middle, and then I had to catch my plane. They made me promise to come back soon if they gave it back. Then I ran across the tarmac and up the stairs to the plane. I thought I wouldn't be back in Belize for years, but I was wrong.

# 4

# TALES AND WARNINGS
# IN THE BUSH

When I returned home, I was surprised to see that news of the race had already been published in the *Toronto Star* as well as in the paper from Oakville, my home town. The day after I had ridden the race, the *Toronto Star* had run the headline "Metro Student Cycles To Stop Jaguar Deaths" and that was how several of my friends had learned that I had finished the race. Other news stories followed, as did radio interviews, and then the activity died down and I settled back into my relatively quiet life in Toronto.

Though I enjoyed the excitement of Belize, it was time to get back to my Master of Science program in zoology at the university. I was ready to begin a series of experiments, using pigeons, on jet-lag, when I found out the equipment I needed would not be available for a year. Unless I wanted to postpone my work, I would have to choose another thesis topic. My supervisor and I discussed several other options, among them that I check out the possibilities of doing research on jaguars in Belize, since I had made good connections there.

I knew that Alan Rabinowitz from the NYZS had just finished his jaguar study in the Cockscomb Basin, so I called him in New York to see if it would be possible for me to work in the Cockscomb. Rabinowitz said he thought I could probably gather enough information on jaguar food habits, parasites and possibly ranges to develop a master's thesis. He also said that the NYZS and the Belize Audubon Society would appreciate my stay since it would be beneficial to have someone living in the reserve to discourage poachers. I would, of course, still have to supply my own source of funding. Rabinowitz was planning to be in the reserve, helping set it up, for about one week every month during the five months I was planning to be there, and he offered to teach me field-work while he was there.

I had little knowledge of the tropics other than my brief visits and even less knowledge on the ecology of the jaguar. But my trips to Belize had been inspiring and I wanted to learn more.

Within weeks of changing my thesis topic to the study of the jaguar, I was packing to go to Belize. Funding was a problem because of the short notice, but World Wildlife Fund (Canada) came through again in the crunch, and supplied me with enough money to set up. I thought I had enough of my own money saved to help with any emergencies that would certainly arise. I set about getting all the required shots and malaria pills, and putting together a good first-aid kit. Even though I had done a lot of wilderness camping in Canada, and hoped that that experience might help, I wasn't exactly sure what to expect.

I had been told to bring long pants and long-sleeved shirts for working in the bush because of the bugs, the sun and the thorny vines. Remembering my sunburn from the race, I packed bottles and bottles of sun block along with my mosquito repellant. I sublet my apartment near the university and spent the last few days packing things to go with me or to put into storage. I stayed up all night organizing and packing last-minute items in the middle of my parents' living-room. As I checked over my list and made sure I had the supplies I needed, Dad said, "Are you sure you know what you're getting yourself into?"

"Not really," I said, "but I'll soon find out!"

I finally finished packing at dawn and I had a few minutes alone with my thoughts. Normally, once I make a decision to do something, I stop worrying about it. But this was a lot more serious than heading off to a summer job, or a new school or anything else I had ever done. For a moment I felt a bit nervous about going, but then I thought about seeing all my friends in Belize again and catching up on the latest cycling news and I realized I wasn't going to some foreign land. I was going back to a familiar place, to friendly people.

Mom and Dad took me to the airport and I promised to write. It would be a few weeks before I realized how important letters from home could be. Though they were kidding around about all the things I took with me, Mom and Dad looked a bit worried. I guess it wasn't easy to have their youngest daughter leave to spend five months in a jungle in Central America. But I was one of six rather strong-willed children, and Mom and Dad had put up with many strange adventures before mine.

I flew to Miami and then transferred onto TACA Airlines to Belize. From the air, Belize seemed like it was all bush, and now that I knew I would be living there, it seemed even more dense than before. Soon I would be down there, tracking the elusive jaguar. It was too late to turn back now.

Soon after I arrived in Belize City, I met with Alan Rabinowitz. I had met him when I first visited the reserve and had spoken to him several times on the telephone about my project. He said that his trip to the Cockscomb this time would be short, only three days. He would be spending most of that time with a forestry officer, who was going into the Cockscomb with us to do a tree survey.

The Belizean government wanted to make sure there were no large trees within the central area of the reserve that could be useful for logging. The basin had previously been logged of mahogany and other useful trees. In fact, the cabin I was to live in while in the Cockscomb was part of the abandoned logging camp that had been active during Rabinowitz's stay there. In the past, the government had made money by leasing the area to loggers. But since the core area of the reserve had already been logged, the government was willing to set aside that area as a zone where all logging was banned as long as no significant trees could be found. In the rest of the reserve, only selective logging of specific trees was to be allowed.

Though the government knew the core area had been logged, it was the job of the forestry officer to go into the Cockscomb and check to make sure that there were few, if any, good, large logging trees left. Together, the forestry officer and Rabinowitz and several of the Mayans were to complete a tree survey of the core area in the three days they were there.

Rabinowitz had rented a Land Rover in which we headed down to the Cockscomb. On the way we picked up Fausdino Sentino, the forestry officer who was to do the tree survey. Fausdino was a soft-spoken Creole man in his late thirties. He didn't want to come with us that week because his wife was expecting a baby at any moment. But Rabinowitz was scheduled to fly back to New York in a few days so the survey had to be done immediately.

Though the drive from Belize City to the Cockscomb is about 125 miles (200 km), it seemed longer in a Land Rover. The first 50 miles (80 km) to Belmopan we covered quickly because the road was mostly paved. The gravel stretches were shorter than they had been on the bike route because much of the construction had been completed. Instead of continuing west after Belmopan, as I had during the race, we turned south onto the Hummingbird Highway, which winds through the Maya Mountains.

The scenery along this stretch of highway is beautiful, but the road was filled with pot-holes and gravel. Most of the bridges were only wide enough for one car at a time, and some of the turns took my breath away. Many of the bridge railings were dented or torn through, where cars or buses hadn't quite made it. I didn't have to worry about the pot-holes because I wasn't driving, so I concentrated on the scenery. The bridges stretched over beautiful creeks and rivers that wound through the mountain valleys. It was like being on a roller-coaster, as the road dipped into a valley, then climbed quickly to the next peak. At the crests of the rolls, the jungle seemed to stretch out forever, winding its way up the steep slopes as far as I could see. Along the road's edge, small settlements and an occasional snack bar would appear every few miles and break up the various shades of green.

A large area of burnt stumps and darkened ground made the reports of jungles being destroyed by slash-and-burn farming seem too real. As the tropical forests disappear, not only the wildlife is lost, but also the dense protection the vegetation provides for the soil. Deforestation often results in serious soil-erosion problems, which frequently cause major floods and contaminate water supplies with silt.

In slash-and-burn farming, first an area is cleared, often by machete, and then set on fire to burn off the rest of the vegetation. The boundaries of the cut area are supposed to stop the fire but frequently do not. Often a larger area is burned than is intended. This decreases the vegetation even more. Though crops are planted in the newly burned area, within a few years the crops falter because the soil in many areas of tropical forest is poor. Then new areas of the forest are slashed and burned to plant the crops.

Belizeans had lived off the land in this manner for years, but now it was happening on a much larger scale, threatening the existence of the tropical forests. Because of the unrest from neighbouring Central American countries, large numbers of illegal immigrants were moving into the less-accessible parts of the tropical forest and starting small farm plots they called "milpas."

The milpas weren't the only cause of deforestation. Farther along the highway, we passed a Hershey chocolate factory and then several orange plantations. These factories had also taken their toll on the jungle. As we approached the Cockscomb we passed several grazing fields that had been stripped of tropical forest and where now only grass and cows could be seen. The tropical forest was fast disappearing, and on each trip I made after this one, I would see less bush and more fields.

The Hummingbird Highway ends in Dangriga Town. Dangriga is a small coastal town with the population consisting mostly of Garifuna and a few Creoles. It was where I would pick up my mail and get supplies about once a week. Dangriga was only about 28 miles (45 km) from the Cockscomb but it took several hours by car because of the bad roads. From the Hummingbird Highway we turned onto the Southern Highway and passed the small settlement of Silkgrass, the location of the nearest telephone – 12.5 miles (20 km) from the Cockscomb.

The Southern Highway is a rough gravel-and-sand road. But because it has never been paved, there are few pot-holes, so it is an improvement over the Hummingbird Highway. We turned off the highway into Maya Centre. This Mayan Indian village of about 25 families, was at the entrance road into the Cockscomb Basin and was its nearest settlement. Ignacio and his son Pedro, the two wardens for the reserve, greeted us near their home at the entrance.

Ignacio and his wife lived in a thatched-roof hut with their many children. Ignacio was a small, but strong man, who had gained his extensive knowledge of the bush through hunting. His skills were now being used to help protect wildlife. Ignacio and Pedro, as part of their duties as wardens, were responsible for keeping the trails cleared in the reserve and for keeping the cabin area clear of tall vegetation. As the vegetation here grew quickly, this was a never-ending job. I would see Ignacio and Pedro at least once a week, when they walked the 6 miles (10 km) in to the cabin area to cut bush with their machetes.

Pedro, age 16, was Ignacio's oldest son and would soon be getting married. Girls in this village and in surrounding Mayan communities didn't wait as long, and many got married at age 13 – the age of Pedro's fiancée.

Ignacio's wife, Adriana, was a short, stout woman in her mid-30s who looked many years older than her true age, no doubt because she had borne ten children (several of them had died) and was expecting another. All the children except one stood in the shade of the thatched roof, shyly looking at the Rover as it came in. Agapita, their eight-year-old daughter, wasn't shy at all and seemed excited at our arrival. She told me, in somewhat broken English, different from the Creole I had grown used to, that everyone called her "Pita" for short and I could too. The village was alive with activity. Many dogs, chickens and children ran in and out of the dirt-floored, thatched-roof huts.

After catching up on the latest news, we left Maya Centre and headed down the narrow dirt road toward the old logging camp, called Quam Bank, which would be my home for the next few months. Quam Bank was 6 miles (10 km) from Maya Centre but it seemed farther because of the rough road that wound around large craters in the ground. These holes had been made with dynamite to destroy the original straight road that was used as a landing strip. I was told this was done to discourage people from growing marijuana in the area, because now planes couldn't land to pick up the crops. As we drove slowly along this rugged road, I kept a sharp look-out for jaguars. I knew sightings were rare but there was always that small chance.

Once we got there, Rabinowitz and Fausdino began their survey and I set about moving into my cabin. It was one of several cabins that had belonged to the logging operation. The camp was now abandoned and there was one other scientist staying there who was finishing off a study in the Cockscomb, but he was away at the moment. Nari, a young Guatemalan, who had been hired to oversee the cabins and sell the wood from the cabins that were rotting, would be there only for a couple more weeks and was staying in a cabin at the edge of the camp.

The cabin I had chosen was very solid, and I soon found out that there weren't many leaks in the roof. It had been empty for a long time, and strange creatures were living under boards and in corners. There were windows in every room, which would be very helpful since there was no electricity in the cabin, even though there obviously had been when the logging camp was in operation, as a lone lightbulb hung from a socket over the bed.

A porcelain bathroom sink was the focal point in the main room. I hadn't expected anything as fancy as that. However, when I scrubbed it clean and rinsed the grit off with a bowl of water, my toes got soaked. The sink drained straight onto the floor! After that I tried to remember to keep a bucket under the sink. There was a long counter nearby – obviously the kitchen area. The bedroom had a large wooden bed frame onto which I could throw a foam mattress, and there were shelves for my clothes.

I would have to get my water from the creek, 218 yards (200 m) down the road. I had seen the Mayan women carrying water on their heads, but later, when I tried that, I spilled more water than I kept. Even after I had had time to practise, I found it easier to balance the bucket on my shoulder than on my head.

The best discovery was a real flush toilet in the back room, which had no door. Though I had to dump a bucket of water into it every time to get it to flush, it still beat going out into the bush in the middle of the night. It wasn't until later that I learned the value of water, and found that the toilet was much more useful during the rainy season when water could be collected from the roof.

After a good clean-up job, I admired my nice little cabin. It was bigger than my tiny apartment back home. There were even screens on the windows. I set up the kerosene stove and got out my groceries. Eating was going to be a problem. I had spent almost three times the money on groceries than I do at home and it was barely enough for the week. Cans of food were expensive in Belize because most of them had to be imported. With no refrigeration and 80°F (26°C) weather, I didn't have much choice. Several weeks later when I was beginning to wonder if I could eat only canned food and rice for five months, someone told me that eggs can keep up to two weeks without refrigeration. This was also a great advantage, since eggs are the cheapest form of protein available.

Ignacio and Pedro arrived at Quam Bank the next morning. They had spotted jaguar tracks on their way in from Maya Centre. They were fresh, made last night. Rabinowitz and I jumped in the Land Rover and headed out to the spot. There were many jaguar tracks just at the edge of the road.

Jaguar tracks look like those of a huge house cat. The claws don't make marks on the ground, as dog nails do, because the cat's claws are retracted when it travels. The jaguar's front feet have five toes, but the first toe is small and set above the others, and it doesn't touch the ground. The back feet have four toes, all of which can be seen in prints. The back feet can usually be distinguished from the front ones in a set of tracks because the front feet are much larger. The example in my tracking book showed one jaguar with a front foot pad that was 4.7 inches (12 cm) wide and a back foot that was only 2.9 inches (7.5 cm) wide, so there was a noticeable difference.

I had read that for communication and to delineate home ranges, jaguars make scrapes, rake trees with their claws, urinate, scent mark, and deposit faeces. These were the signs I would be looking for in my tracking. (Jaguars also use head rubbing to leave scent marks.)

I would be doing most of my field-work alone, so I decided to concentrate my research on tracking jaguars on foot. By measuring track sizes and picking up scats (droppings), it would be possible to determine some basic natural-history information about the jaguars in the Cockscomb Basin. If tracking conditions were good, I might be able to get some idea of minimum home-range sizes. The droppings would be most helpful in determining what the jaguars were eating and what intestinal parasites they carried. Though little was known about the function of scrapes made on the ground, except that they might be territorial signs, I would also record any scrapes I found on the trails.

That day the tracks we found on the side of the road were set deep in mud and so were well defined. I hadn't done any tracking before, but I would soon learn how rare it was to find such perfect tracks. It was easy to re-enact the scene from the muddy evidence that was left behind. A jaguar had come across a paca (a large rodent about the size of a small spaniel) and started the chase. From the criss-crossing of tracks, it was obvious that the jaguar had chased the paca around in circles and then they had both dashed off into the bush. From the sliding marks of both sets of tracks, it had obviously been a high-speed chase. The tracks led off into the tall grass by the edge of the road where they could not be seen. I wondered if the paca had gained his freedom or if the jaguar had captured his meal.

Rabinowitz showed me how to take the required measurements, and I recorded them in my data book. On the way back toward Quam Bank, Rabinowitz warned me that living here would be difficult. He said living in the Cockscomb had aged him ten years and would likely do the same to me. I was surprised he felt that way. I knew there were dangers here, as there were in most field situations, but so far I was glad I had come. There would be times that I wished I was back home, but I was always glad when that wish wasn't granted.

Rabinowitz and Fausdino were ready to leave the next day, the latter convinced that there were no good logging opportunities at the centre of the reserve. That was good news for the reserve, as now even selective logging would be banned in the core area. It would now be safe from official outside intrusion.

I got a ride back to Belize City with Rabinowitz and Fausdino because I wanted to arrange for long-term rental of a Land Rover. I had not planned for this in my budget, since Rabinowitz had said a vehicle was not necessary. But I felt uncomfortable being so isolated without a radio to call out on or a vehicle. Rabinowitz had had a vehicle while he was working in the Cockscomb, and now that the logging camp was not in operation, it was even more necessary. A very rickety motorcycle was available for me to use, but I was warned it needed constant repairs and that its front brakes didn't work at all. In the end, I used up most of the money I had brought down with me to rent my Land Rover.

While the Land Rover was being tuned up, the rental agent lent me his Ford LTD to get some supplies. A young American woman, Sue, who was visiting Belize came with me and we parked the car on a side street and went to the only pizza place in Belize. After ordering, I noticed two young, scruffy-looking men sitting at the other table.

I noticed them because they were conspicuously not noticing us. In Belize I had gotten used to being looked at because my appearance was so different from that of most people there. Usually that was helpful because people that I had met only once would recognize me. Even people I had never met, but who had seen me in the papers, would come up and talk to me about jaguars. It was a wonderful way of making new friends and of learning more about jaguars.

These two young men in the pizza parlour had certainly not recognized me, but had instead decided Sue and I were tourists. They left a minute before we did, and I noticed we passed them on the street. We walked back to the car and I started it up. As I rolled down the power window, one of the guys from the pizza place approached my car. I thought he was going to ask me if I wanted to buy some coral or something. Instead he leaned on the window edge and said, "Gimmee dat," gesturing with his head to my purse sitting on the seat beside me. I, of course, said no. Not only did my purse contain some money, but also my track data book. There was no way he was getting that!

He repeated his request and pulled out a long hunting knife and held it shakily between my eyes. He was wavering it a bit too much, so I reached up and grabbed the base of the blade, which luckily wasn't sharp. I didn't try to move the knife. I just tried to hold it still, so that he wouldn't hit my eye by accident.

I had always wondered what I'd do in a situation like this, but my reaction surprised him as well as me: I got angry, very angry. I was insulted that this guy didn't recognize me from the bike race. Not only was he trying to take my data book, but he was making me doubt the efficacy of the bike race's P.R. campaign!

Belize is not a violent country, but because there are so few tourists, the likelihood of their being robbed is greater. Tourists are known to carry cash, and robbers have found that if they leave passports, traveller's cheques and everything else except cash at the scene of the crime, the tourists will not wait the few months necessary to take them to court.

Anyway I said, "No way! Get out of here!" He didn't. Then I switched to yelling at him in Creole, in the hope that he would realize I was local and leave me alone. He did look surprised and worried, but kept the knife in my face. I told Sue to put the car in drive, because I couldn't move my hands for fear he would cut my face. She put the car in drive from the passenger seat, and it picked up speed slowly. Our robber started jogging beside the car and I couldn't steer because both my hands were on the knife blade. I gave a big push and gunned the car. He was left behind. I could see him running away in my rear-view mirror.

The car shot up to the corner, which was only a few yards away, and I jumped out and yelled to a policeman standing across the street. He ran in the direction the robber had run, and Sue and I headed to the police station. When we finally had a chance to talk, Sue said, "Your face is cut, near your eye! Does it hurt?" I hadn't noticed anything, and was surprised that, when I touched the spot, it stung. The cut was a couple of inches long, but was not deep, more like a paper cut. It was fortunate that it had missed my eye. Lucky again!

Sue did not fare so well. I hadn't realized it, but while I was hanging on to the knife for dear life, the other guy had reached into the car on her side and grabbed her purse. She had lost her passport and sixty dollars. The policeman came back with Sue's purse in his hand. The guy had dropped it and run. As expected, the money was gone, but her passport was there. I gave her thirty dollars. Either of us could have been robbed, and while a thirty dollar loss was not too bad, neither of us could afford to lose sixty dollars.

We drove to the police station and, while we were reporting the robbery, they brought in the man who had held the knife to my face. I filled out the reports, but since Sue had to leave Belize before the trial, she could not press charges.

I dropped Sue off at her hotel, and went back to the small guest house I was staying at. Errol, Turhan and Adrian dropped by, and I told them about the robbery. They said the mugger would get out on bail that afternoon, and I was worried that he might come after me. But they said that that would be the last thing he would do. Thieves didn't get much time for their crimes, they said, but if anything happened to me after he was charged, he would be put in jail for a long time. They also assured me that the robber would have found out who I was by now and that I had lots of friends in Belize City. (They never did catch the other robber, but later at the trial this one was sentenced to one year in jail for robbery and one year for wounding.)

After my friends left, I went over to the Fort George Hotel for a swim in the pool. It was just closing and I sat out by the pool, talking to an elderly American gentleman. He had heard about the jaguar reserve and was interested, so we talked for quite some time. Suddenly a young Belizean man who was always causing trouble around town showed up beside us. He was trying to sell us coral, and I said we didn't want any. He had been drinking and started to get angry. I was getting nervous because it was dark out by the pool, and since the pool was closed, there was no security guard. I started to worry whether he was carrying a knife. I became so scared that I couldn't move, and couldn't say a word. I finally told him that the elderly man and I would take a look at the coral tomorrow morning, but we had no money with us now.

After he left, I realized I was shaking and I couldn't stop. It was probably a delayed reaction from the mugging. I went into the hotel lounge to calm myself down before I drove back to the guest house where I was staying that night. It had finally dawned on me that I could have been killed for refusing to give up my purse with the tracking book in it. I had been lucky, but I had also been stupid.

I was still feeling panicked and staring into my lemonade, when one of the managers came over and asked me if I was okay. I said I was fine, but I wanted to go home. He said, "You can't drive all the way back to the Cockscomb tonight." I said, "No. I mean my real home – Canada. I can't stay here any more." He looked concerned and pulled up a chair and said, "Of all the people I've met, I never thought I'd hear you say that. Belize is your home now."

I explained to him what had happened, and it made me feel better to talk about it. He told me that there were very few dangerous people in Belize, and that foreigners did stand out. That was why I was much more likely to encounter danger than most people here. In fact Belize was probably much less dangerous than Toronto.

I had parked my car on a back street, and it was now pitch-black outside, so I was afraid to go to it. I asked the manager if I could just leave it there for the night and come back for it the next day. He said, "What happened to the girl who's not afraid of anything?" I laughed, and said, "She's having a bad night." He walked me to the car to make sure I got off safely. Before I drove off, he said quietly, "We're not all bad you know." I felt sorry that he thought I was angry with all Belizeans. I had just had a little more than I could take in one day. "I know," I replied. "I'll be okay tomorrow. Thanks for everything." I drove back to the guest house for the night.

The next day, I did feel much better. It was good to get my Land Rover back. It made me look less like a tourist than the LTD had, and it was much more useful.

I spent too much money on groceries again, and then picked up some pigtail buckets. These large white buckets are used for everything imaginable in Belize. They are used to carry water from rivers and pipes, to mix up punch at large gatherings, to collect oranges and peanuts in the fields, to cover small plants during a heavy rain, to use as an extra stool around the house or to hold a child's toys. But first they are used to import pigtails.

Salted pigtails are popular because they are one of the few meats that can be kept unrefrigerated for long periods of time. Pigtails can be bought one at a time and, when stewed with vegetables, can be stretched a long way. I told one of the Belizean cyclists I knew that they sounded pretty awful, and he was amazed we didn't eat them in Canada. I said I'd never heard of them before, and asked him where they were imported from. He read the fine print on the label and looked up at me, grinning. That bucket was exported to Belize from Toronto!

I managed to scrounge a few empty buckets at the market. The lids sealed well, which made the buckets useful for storing camera equipment and film. They were also good for carrying water up to the cabin from the creek. It was also important for me to have a sealed bucket for my bags of dried jaguar droppings. Otherwise living in the cabin with jaguar scats could become quite unbearable.

I started back down to the Cockscomb, picking up hitch-hikers as I went. I had been warned not to offer rides to strangers, but with my Land Rover I could lock myself in the front cab and seat the people I picked up in the back. This made it all reasonably safe, as long as the Rover didn't break down at an isolated spot on the highway. I always stopped at a snack bar part-way down the Hummingbird Highway called Over-the-Top Cool Spot, and this time the lady running it scolded me when she saw six people jump out of the back of the Rover. "It's dangerous to pick up people on the side of the road. Most people are nice enough, but it only takes one . . ."

One of the guys I picked up came over and told me the same thing. I laughed and told him if I hadn't offered him a ride, he would be still sitting on the road, miles back. Suddenly his face lit up, "Wait a

minute, I know you! I rode with you part-way in the Cross-Country!"
He was the guy who had waited to push me up the hill. I had thought
he looked familiar when I had picked him up, but my memories of
parts of the race were a bit fuzzy. No longer a stranger, he sat in the
front with me for the next part of the drive, and we laughed about the
bike race.

I was glad he was there because a few miles later I got the first of
many flat tires in Belize. He showed me how to fix a flat quickly, and
pointed out several houses along the route where people would patch a
tire in case I got two flats. This information would prove useful, since
two flats along this stretch would later be a common occurrence for
me.

It was good to get back to the Cockscomb again and especially nice to
be on my own. I was a bit nervous, but now I could finally get started.
Rabinowitz was to return in three weeks and had suggested it would
take a while for me to get settled and used to living there. Then when
he returned, we could begin organized field-work.

In fact, Rabinowitz's contract was repeatedly postponed and he did
not return to Belize at all while I was there. If I had known at the
outset that that was to happen, I never would have agreed to come to
the Cockscomb. Thank goodness I didn't find out until it was too late
to change my mind.

I spent most of the day sorting through my equipment and putting
everything away. I had discovered that it got dark at about 6:00 p.m.,
and flashlight batteries could be saved if I remembered where
everything was. After dark, I heated up a can of beans on my
one-burner pump kerosene stove. It took me a while to figure out
exactly how the stove worked, and I managed to have some quite
impressive flames shooting up to the wood ceiling at one point.
Finally I got the stove working without burning anything important.
By the time the beans were heated, I was hungry enough that they
tasted good. Then I heated a bit of water and washed up the dishes in
the sink. This time I remembered to put the bucket underneath when
I drained the sink. I was beginning to sort out my routine.

Then I tried to read. It was difficult to read by candlelight and the
little storm lanterns weren't much better. Reading was possible when
necessary, but hard on my eyes and definitely not something that I

could spend hours a night doing. It was only then that I realized how long the nights could be.

At 8:30 I decided to get some sleep. I was just nodding off when I heard voices, and saw a light coming toward my cabin along the trail. Nari had returned to the Cockscomb while I was in Belize City. But the voices weren't coming from Nari's cabin and as far as I knew he was the only other person here. I quickly got dressed and waited in the darkness in the cabin. "Hello! Hello!" I heard as the light approached; I saw it was a Mayan Indian and his young son. Relieved, I let them in and we sat by their lamp in the cabin.

He introduced himself as Gregorio from Maya Centre and told me he was working for Nari, taking down some of the cabins. He explained that he would be finished with the job soon, and wondered if I had any work for him. I told him that I had no money, and would be doing everything on my own. Though he was disappointed, he stayed to chat. His seven-year-old son, Francisco, sat bright-eyed and silent in the lamplight beside him.

Nari must have heard the voices and soon he too joined us. Gregorio was a shy, quiet man, but Nari was the complete opposite. I didn't know much about Nari, but what I had seen so far hadn't impressed me. I had a hunch that he lied whenever it was convenient and often contradicted himself within a conversation. This particular night he was enjoying telling me about all the things that could harm me in the jungle. He seemed disappointed that I did not quake over his animated tale of the hairy apeman who would kill men and carry women off into the bushes. Gregorio added details to spice up the story.

Meanwhile, Francisco sat like a kid at camp, leaning forward in his chair with excitement. We heard about the *duende*, a small four-fingered elf-like creature that can help or harm those that it encounters. According to legend, if it sees that you have five fingers it will get angry and rip off your thumb or lose you in the jungle, but if you hide your thumb it will teach you to play a musical instrument. When they saw I wasn't terrified, they told me that Rabinowitz had said he saw what he thought was a *duende* while he was working at night in the bush.

I found the tales more entertaining than frightening, until Nari started talking about the real dangers of the bush. The Cockscomb was known for its abundant snakes, especially the deadly fer de lance. One of Rabinowitz's assistants had been killed by a fer de lance in the Cockscomb. That snake had been more than 6 feet (2 m) long. Nari had graphic descriptions of other people who had been bitten and had died painful deaths from fer de lance bites. Gregorio also knew several people who had been bitten by snakes, but said not all of them had died. He used the term "tommygoff" for the fer de lance, but Nari said a "tommygoff" was any snake. "Yellow-jawed tommygoff" was the specific term for the fer de lance because the snake had yellow on its throat. Nari told us to put garlic on our boots or shoes and on our pants up to the knees to keep the fer de lance away. I never did try that. Gregorio and Nari both told me to kill approaching snakes with a machete. Ha! I was still having trouble hitting inanimate objects with my machete.

Rabinowtiz had left me fer de lance antivenin that I was to carry with me on the trail in case I was bitten. If you are bitten and poison is injected into your system, and if antivenin is not used, death can occur within hours from massive internal bleeding. But, after reading the package, I wasn't sure I wanted to use it. Antivenin is made from the blood serum of horses and can cause severe allergic reactions in many people. If bitten you should test for allergy by putting a drop of the antivenin in your eye and waiting to see if the eye turns red. If it does, it means you are allergic to the horse serum and should not use it. If you are allergic to the antivenin you can die from anaphylactic shock within minutes of injecting it, because the antivenin will cause your blood vessels to leak and your blood pressure to drop. If that doesn't kill you, your breathing passages can swell up and cause suffocation. If you are not allergic, though, the antivenin could save your life by inactivating the snake's venom.

It sounded to me like a game of Russian roulette with a needle. Snakes sometimes bite and inject little or no poison, so before injecting antivenin you must wait until you feel the effect of the poison. Even if the snake has injected poison, it is possible that it will not cause death. Another problem is determining what species of snake has bitten you. The snake could bite the back of your leg and then disappear into the bush before you could identify it.

Somehow I couldn't imagine myself sitting in the bush after being bitten by a fer de lance, trying to tell if my own eye was red and then

*Preceding page: Panthera onca.* The largest cat on the continent faces extinction.

*Above:* On top of a Mayan temple, overlooking the Temple of the Jaguar in Tikal, Guatemala.

*Left:* Looking down at Cockscomb Basin, with Quam Bank in clearing.

*Above:* Adrian, Errol and Turhan before one of our training rides.

*Right:* After finishing the cross-country classic bike race.

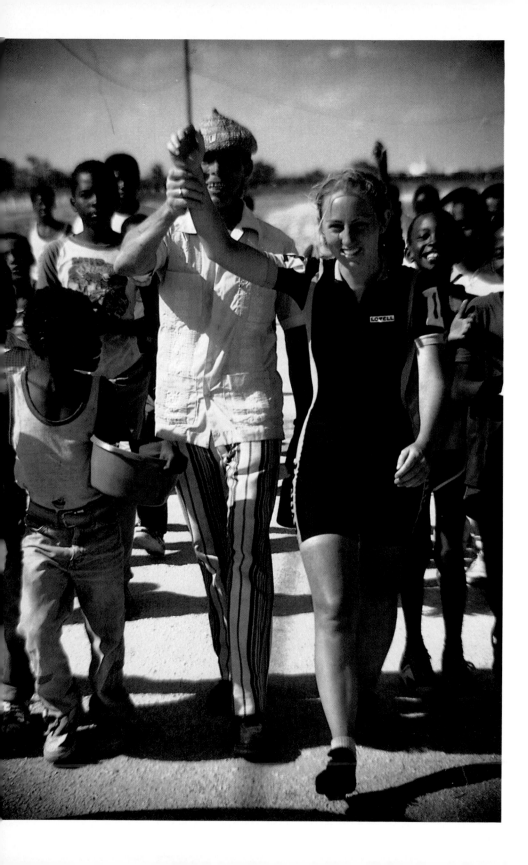

*Top:* Cockscomb wardens, Ignacio and Pedro erecting sign at Quam Bank.

*Above Right:* Down the Hummingbird Highway.

*Right:* The main street in Dangriga.

*Above:* Children play at Maya Centre while babies rest in white hammocks. Road into Cockscomb in background.

*Above Right:* Ignacio and family, along with Vincent, at Maya Centre.

*Right:* My cabin with buckets to catch water from roof. Tigger foreground.

*Left:* Though jaguars are large, their coat helps them blend into their surroundings, making them difficult to see.

*Above Right:* Tracks of a jaguar chasing a paca.

*Centre Right:* Jaguar scrape.

*Below Right:* In Belize, people, as well as jaguars, enjoy eating iguanas.

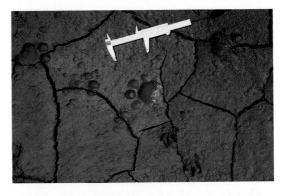

My truck being rescued from the river.

e watching Pollyanna from the stand the jaguar later jumped under.

*Above:* John Mackie and Ignacio at Dangriga airstrip.

*Right:* Prince Philip bird-watching in Cockscomb.

*Overleaf:* The jaguar is now protected in the Cockscomb Basin, but in other parts of it
range, it is rapidly disappearing as tropical forests are destroyed.

trying to remember what the snake looked like, and then deciding that I was now sick enough to take the antivenin and then continuing to inject myself until I got to Maya Centre (which would take several hours), all the while being deathly ill. It seemed to me that it would be safer to take my chances with the snake poison.

Nari and Gregorio continued their reports on snakes for some time, and then switched to explaining how herds of peccaries could kill a person alone on the trail if they were upset. Jaguars (which they called tigers) were also extremely dangerous and could kill a person in an instant, Nari explained, but only when they were hungry. I asked them both if they knew of anyone who had been killed or hurt by a jaguar and their response was silence. Neither of them had ever heard of anyone being hurt by a jaguar. In sharp contrast to the snakes, jaguars appeared to be much less dangerous to people. That was the first bit of encouraging news I had heard all evening!

Nari said that jaguars weren't always afraid of people. His brother had been driving a front-end loader one day, when a jaguar appeared ahead of him on the road. His brother moved right up to the jaguar and raised the shovel to squash the cat, and the jaguar barely stepped out of the way in time. It moved slowly and didn't seem to be afraid. Why anyone would want to squash a jaguar with a front-end loader was beyond me, but this story was a bit odd even for Nari to have made up.

I had heard similar stories about jaguars' lack of fear when I was in Belize City. One of the cyclists had told me that he knew a man who had been out hunting when he killed a paca, or "gibnut" as they say in Creole. He set the carcass by a tree and continued hunting for several hours. When he returned and reached behind the tree to grab the carcass, his hand hit something big. He stepped around the tree, and found a jaguar sitting over the half-eaten paca. At the same time that he swung his machete at the jaguar, the cat lashed out at him in surprise. Both received only superficial blows and ran off in opposite directions. The hunter came back and picked up the carcass and took it home. He still has the scar on his chest from the encounter. Like most fishing stories, hunting stories are more fiction than fact, but usually based at least loosely on the latter.

After several more tales, Nari and Gregorio headed out of the cabin into the night. I called after them to be careful of the hairy apeman and they laughed, but I noticed Francisco was sticking closer to his father's side now.

I woke up just before dawn and made breakfast in the dark. I wanted to be out on the trail at first light. I packed some Ziplock bags in my day backpack in case I found any faeces, and some plaster of Paris to make casts of tracks. I also took measuring callipers, sun-tan lotion, mosquito repellant, some food, and my camera and film. It was barely dawn when I set out down an overgrown logging road. It was misty and cool and the jungle looked beautiful, mysterious and peaceful.

The bush was incredibly dense in some areas and I was amazed at how quickly it had regrown. In 1961, the Cockscomb Basin, an area of about 150 square miles (400 km$^2$) had been hit hard by a hurricane. It had also been logged extensively. Because of the climate and amount of rainfall, the recovery had been quite fast. Much of the basin is secondary-growth broadleaf forest, and the undergrowth is very dense. Already the top of the canopy was about 65 to 80 feet (20 to 25 m) high in most areas.

Cohune palms are the most common trees in the Cockscomb, but the variety of tree species is impressive. More than 200 different tree species can be found in the basin. Vines are everywhere and make it difficult to tell where one tree stops and another begins. Many of the vines have spines and prickles that would catch on my skin or clothes as I walked. I soon learned to recognize which ones hurt the most and to try to avoid them. The local names for these vines such as "haul-em-back" and "tear-me-coat," seemed much more appropriate than the scientific ones.

In some spots a huge tree that escaped logging saws and the hurricane would stick up above the canopy. Epiphytes, plants that grow supported by other plants, grew in most junctions of branches and trunk. The epiphytes were more common in the older trees and so were not as abundant in the Cockscomb. Along the river banks were rows and rows of dumb cane, a plant that looks much like sugar cane. It thrives in areas that frequently flood. The variations in shape and shade of green were amazing and made the jungle look like a tumbled interlocking mass of leaves and branches.

Leaf-cutting ants, or "wee wee ants" as they are called locally, were busy doing their best at gardening. At frequent intervals along the trail, I would have to step over a line of ants, each individual ant carrying a leaf or piece of leaf that was many times its size. Sometimes the doomed plant would be right on the trail edge and I could watch as they cut piece after piece off each leaf.

I had put on mosquito repellant before I left the cabin, but the bugs didn't seem too bad. They were worst just before dusk, but by then I would be in the cabin. Even at their worst, the bugs didn't seem as annoying as those one meets when camping in Northern Ontario. I wasn't too worried about the insect bites themselves, but about the little "extras" that might accompany them. I knew I was reasonably safe from malaria as long as I took my foul-tasting malaria pills once a week, but I could do nothing to protect myself from the disgusting botfly larvae.

Botflies lay their eggs on mosquitoes and when such a laden mosquito lands on a person's skin, the heat hatches the eggs and the tiny larvae fall onto the human. They burrow into the skin and live by eating your flesh! Once the botfly gets large enough to cause pain, it is usually discovered, but is not easy to remove. It must breathe through a hole in the surface of your skin, so it is often possible to see the top end of it. Unfortunately, the other end has tiny hooks that dig in deeper if you try to pull the botfly out.

There are many suggested methods of removal, from squeezing below the area with pliers (which may cause the parasite to burst and so infect the area), to sticking a piece of meat over the hole and hoping the botfly will burrow through the meat to get to the surface. Gregorio had suggested that the best method is to make a poultice out of tobacco leaves and cover the hole. The tobacco would kill the larvae, which could then be squeezed out. Every time I felt a mosquito bite me, I would wonder if I was soon to become part of an interesting parasite study. But luckily I never did become a botfly host.

As I continued along the trail, I noticed that it was starting to get warmer, though it was still bearable. I had my machete in a casing hanging from my belt and I was beginning to realize how awkward it was going to be to carry it all the time. I'm shorter than most people, and it hung down to the middle of my calf. Every time I took a step, the machete hit my leg. I was walking forward, trying to adjust it, when I heard an animal slide off the trail just in front of me. I looked up quickly and glimpsed a reptile's tail disappearing into the bush. I froze.

The previous night's stories of slow death by snake bite flooded back to me. Then I realized that this stupid machete might be useful after all! It did make me feel better, holding it in my hand. I stood, not moving, with my machete raised until my arm ached. Whatever was in the bushes was not moving anymore so I sidled by, facing the spot it had been, with my machete ready. Nothing jumped out of the bush at me, so I relaxed a bit and kept going along the trail. Just as I was beginning to enjoy myself again, I heard another noise and saw a tail slide into the bushes.

This was not a pleasant situation. If I wanted to keep going, I would have to pass whatever was just off the trail. And if I wanted to give up and go back to the cabin, I would have to pass whatever had jumped off the trail back there. I decided that I had better keep going forward, or face the fact that I couldn't do my research in the Cockscomb. I convinced myself that the last little bit of tail had looked more like a lizard's, and they were harmless. I was still cautious when I passed by where it had entered the bush.

I kept walking along the trail, trying to concentrate on looking for jaguar signs. There were a few more noises and tail flashes, but I could hear them move far off the trail. It was starting to get hot, so I put on some more suntan lotion. As I rounded a corner in the trail, a 6-foot (2-m) snake zipped across the trail immediately in front of me. I jumped backward and then stayed perfectly still, trying to hear something that would tell me which direction it was headed, but there was silence. Slowly, I backed down the trail, away from the spot where it had entered the bush. Now I was scared. My panic had conveniently dulled my senses and I could not recall even what colour the snake was. I tried to reason with myself that it was probably a harmless variety, but I couldn't quite convince myself. I returned to the cabin, jumping at every slight movement in the bush.

It took me a while to settle the argument that was going on in my head. Part of me was ready to pack my suitcases, and the other part was ready to go back on the trail again. I sat in the cabin a long time and tried to figure out what I was really afraid of. The worst thing that could happen was that I would die of snake poison out on the trail. At home, I drove a car, even though I could be killed in a car accident. The chances were slightly higher here, but thousands of people have survived, living in the jungle.

I felt a bit better after thinking things through, and I decided I had better go back on the trail right away before I lost my nerve again. This time I watched a bit farther ahead and soon became good at spotting lizards before they dove into the bush. Most of the scurrying noises were harmless lizards, and, if I saw them before I heard them, it made me feel better. After a while, I could tell the difference between a lizard running into the bush and a snake, just by hearing the foliage move.

The Cockscomb looked beautiful to me again. Exotic-looking birds were flitting across the trail, and I even found some faded jaguar tracks! I decided to carry my large knife instead of my machete, which made walking more enjoyable. I was still a bit nervous, but it helped to think of tracking as a challenge rather than a threat.

I had had no experience tracking animals before I came to the Cockscomb and it was difficult, if not impossible, to tell individual jaguars apart by their tracks. The consistency of the mud and sand and the type of substrate were so variable in the Cockscomb, that it was difficult to compare tracks found in one area with those found elsewhere. Hardening mud made tracks look very different from ones made in sandy gravel, and even when I could follow tracks along a trail and see that they had been made by the same jaguar, it was hard to believe because of the differences in the measurements when the substrate changed.

When I first started walking the trails, looking for tracks, I would often miss everything that wasn't a complete paw print. Whenever Ignacio and Pedro would walk in from Maya Centre, they would tell me if they had seen any tracks on the roadway. More often than not, they had found something, but frequently, just a single toe print. It amazed me that they could walk so fast and still see a slight indentation in the sand that was about the size of a penny. Whenever I found tracks near the cabin, I would show Ignacio when he came by, and he would explain how old he thought they were, based on the sharpness of the edges and the recent weather conditions. Soon I was making estimates of my own, and they were matching his with more accuracy. I knew that I would never be able to track as well as Ignacio, because he had grown up reading the ground the way that I had grown up reading books.

Cougar tracks were very difficult to distinguish from jaguar tracks. I had been told that cougar toe prints were more elliptical in shape and that the back of the paw pad was not as round as a jaguar's, but there was some overlap in shape. Though I understood what the differences were supposed to look like, it was often difficult to tell, especially when a track had elliptical toes and a round pad, or some other confusing combination.

Jaguar sightings were fairly common, but cougar sightings rare, in the Cockscomb. The cougar reportedly prefers high ground (hence the name, mountain lion), while the jaguar prefers wet areas, such as the Cockscomb Basin. Jaguars and cougars have also been reported to avoid each other, and this too meant that almost all of the tracks I found were likely those of jaguars.

Then one day I found what I thought were the perfect cougar tracks: they had long, narrow elliptical toes, and the back of the pad was not round at all, but uneven and well defined. I wrote down their exact location on the entrance road into the reserve and headed back to Quam Bank to get my measuring callipers.

When I got to Quam Bank, I saw a vehicle parked by my cabin and found two visitors just walking back to their truck. They were extremely excited because they had seen a jaguar on their drive into the reserve. They described where they had seen it and suddenly I realized that was exactly where I had found the fresh perfect cougar tracks. I couldn't argue with a live sighting. I wasn't sure if this meant I was a bad tracker or if there was a good deal of overlap between the two species. I had just gotten into the Rover to go photograph and measure the tracks when I got caught in a downpour. I sat in the Rover, watching the rain wash all traces of the tracks away.

On my next trip to Belize City, I decided to visit Bader Hassan, a jaguar hunter who lived north of the city, hoping he could give me some pointers on tracking. Bader was a Belizean of Lebanese extraction who was well-known throughout Belize for his skill at hunting jaguars. In the years before 1974, when jaguar hunting was legal in Belize, he would take hunters from all over the world on hunts for the elusive jaguar. He still had a well-trained pack of hunting dogs that he used when he was called in to go after cattle-killing jaguars.

When I got to Bader's house, I was glad he was expecting me. Otherwise I would not have ventured through the pack of tough-looking dogs viciously barking at the Rover. They were a variety of sizes and shapes: a bulldog, several hounds and a huge dog that was mostly Great Dane. When Bader came out of the house to greet me, the dogs calmed down immediately. The Great Dane almost bowled me over as I got out of the Rover. It was almost as tall as I was, and now seemed quite friendly. Bader was a strong, stocky man in his 40s who had an air of confidence about him. As we walked around the back of the house, I noticed two large cages in the backyard. Bader had a captive jaguar and a cougar. Maybe he could show me the differences between the tracks of the two species.

Bader's wife, Mary Ann, an American woman, came out of the house and immediately asked me if I wanted to see the cats. She said they had raised both cats since they were cubs, but the jaguar was never really tame. I had talked to a zoo vet before I came to Belize and he had told me that jaguars are one of the most difficult animals to work with. Other jaguar owners I would later talk to would also tell me that once their jaguars were full grown, they no longer felt safe with them. The oldest jaguar I ever approached was one that had been hand-raised and trained in Ontario by John Rehmann of Vanishing Kingdom. It was about a year old and though it was tame enough then, I wouldn't go into the cage with it when it was a few months older because it had become less predictable.

Bader's jaguar was staring back at me like a wild animal. It was difficult to believe it had been raised in captivity. The dogs came with us toward the cages and barked at both cats, causing the jaguar to lunge at them and hit the cage. Mary Ann told me that the jaguar had been brought to her as a cub by a boy who had hit it with his bicycle. She said that she couldn't understand why the jaguar was so vicious.

Though the cougar was beautiful, it was the jaguar that held my attention. Its spotted coat was so magnificent that I could see why it had been so popular during the fur trade. I was immediately aware of the power of this cat. Its short, thick legs were well-muscled and developed for ambushing its prey. Its head and chest were massive and almost seemed too large for its body. Even its tail was shorter and thicker than those of most other cat species. It was pacing back and forth in the cage, wanting to get to the dogs.

Though I knew it was usually impossible to return hand-raised animals to the wild, I had a feeling that this one was wild enough that it might have a chance. I had a strong urge to set it free, but I knew it was impractical. I was a guest at Bader's home, and if that alone wasn't reason enough, I knew that Bader and his dogs could track this jaguar anywhere it went. Because the jaguar had been hand-raised, it might be aggressive toward humans or associate them with food. It was frustrating to think that such a powerful, aggressive, beautiful cat would likely spend the rest of its life in a metal cage instead of in the jungle. As we moved from its cage toward the cougar's, the jaguar stared back at us through the bars, and for a moment I was glad the bars were there to protect us from the huge cat.

The cougar was the complete opposite. The Baders also had raised it since it was very young, but the cougar was tame enough to live in the house and often travelled with them on a leash. Even though it had been full grown for quite some time, they had only recently caged it. Mary Ann walked right into the cougar's cage and rubbed its head and play-wrestled it. I asked her if she thought it was safe for me to come in too, and she said, "Sure, this cat's very tame." I walked into the cage, and at first the cougar ignored me.

For several minutes I stood and observed the differences between cougars and jaguars. Until now I had only read about them. Though these two cats were about the same size, the cougar was much more agile-looking, but looked much less powerful than did the jaguar. The cougar's soft beige coat was not nearly as arresting as the jaguar's complex markings. Ironically, as the beauty of the jaguar's coat had nearly caused its extinction, the lack of markings on the cougar's fur had provided it with some protection from the fashion industry. The cougar's head was small in comparison, and its tail was longer and more slender.

My comparisons were interrupted as the cougar came toward me and rubbed against my thigh, much like a house cat would rub against a person's calf. It weighed almost as much as I did and I had to brace myself against its weight. Then it started to lick my arm enthusiastically. Its tongue was like thick, wet sandpaper and it made my arm feel raw. I pushed its head over a bit, so at least it wouldn't keep licking the same spot. I rubbed its head and then we tried to leave the cage, but it kept standing between us and the door because it wanted us to stay.

Finally we got out of the cage, and Bader suggested he take the cougar out on a leash and walk it through some mud, so I could see its tracks. Mary Ann handed me the leash and went back in the house, and Bader went in with the cougar. He wrestled with it a bit and then asked me to hand him the leash. I opened the door a crack to hand the leash through and too late saw the cougar's eyes light up. It hit the door at full speed and knocked me backward.

One dog had been sitting outside the cougar's cage, barking at it for several moments. The cougar headed straight for that dog and, before it knew what had happened, the cougar swung and hit it across the head. The dog yelped and ran, and I was amazed that it was still alive. When we looked at it afterward, nothing but its pride was hurt. The cougar had not used its claws or its full power.

The cougar barely slowed down after it hit the dog. It jumped the fence with no effort at all and bolted across the next field. Bader ran one way and I, the other, to cut it off. We chased it for a few minutes and then Bader got close enough to grab its tail and then its collar. He put the leash on and walked it through some mud and then back to its cage.

It was then I noticed that several workers who had been in the yard had vanished. Several moments after Bader put the cougar back in the cage, they returned. "Tame or not," said one woman, "I wouldn't chase after a red tiger." In Belize, jaguars are often called "tigers," and cougars, "red tigers." Ocelots and margays, the smaller spotted cats, are usually called "tiger cats."

Bader and I went back to look at the tracks, which were very clear because of the soft mud. Bader said that the toes were longer and there were three humps on the back of the pad and three on the front, unlike the jaguar's which usually has two. It wasn't always possible to tell them apart, especially when tracking conditions weren't good.

We walked into the house and though I knew Bader was a big-game hunter, I couldn't help but be shocked. The house was filled with animal skins. A stuffed and mounted ocelot was staring back at me from across the room. A zebra rug and jaguar and other skins filled almost every chair and floor space in the house.

Bader was a professional hunter and, though I don't agree with hunting for sport, I wanted to learn what he must know from hunting jaguars. He showed me photographs of several jaguars he killed when hunting was still legal in Belize. He showed me a photograph of a huge jaguar that he had killed more recently because it had killed about 40 cows. It was by far the largest jaguar I had ever seen, and Bader said it had weighed about 250 pounds (113 kg). As usual, he had used his dogs to track the jaguar from a fresh livestock kill. They had chased the cat until it sought refuge in a tree. Then Bader killed it with a single shot.

Bader also told me that many jaguars were unjustly blamed for killing cows. He said he would often get called in to an area where cows had disappeared or died of unknown causes and be told to kill the jaguar that had done it. Often the cows had died from natural causes, such as disease or snake bites, and the jaguar had been found feeding on the dead carcass. In one such case, Bader said he had been called in to a Mennonite community in Belize because a cow had been killed. After examining the carcass he realized that the cow had been killed by a pack of dogs. Though he told them that a jaguar was not responsible, they said that they would often find jaguar tracks in the area and wanted him to kill it before it started to cause trouble. Bader refused, even though he would have been paid well for his trouble. Bader told me about other hunts and about other areas in Belize where jaguars were common.

When I asked him if he thought jaguars were relatively common in the Cockscomb, he said, "Yes, but not nearly as common as the snakes. The one thing about the Cockscomb is that it is crawling with snakes, especially fer de lance. You had better watch where you step!" With those words of warning, I headed back to Belize City.

Back in the city, I met another hunter who had once gone after jaguars. Darryl Adams, a Texan, was in Belize for a fishing trip. He ran a hunting lodge in Mexico, and had hunted many jaguars before they became protected by law. He said he could still make $10,000 for taking people out on a jaguar hunt, but he didn't think it would be right. He hoped that with the ban on hunting they might once again increase their numbers. I asked him why there was such a big demand to hunt jaguars, even though it was now illegal, and people *knew* it was illegal. He said, "One of the biggest problems for the jaguars in Mexico is that the jaguar is listed as a big-game animal of North America. Many big-game hunters want to kill each of the animals on the big-game animal list. They work through the list, one animal at a time, until finally they have killed almost everything on the list except a jaguar. Because there are no jaguars left in the States, the only place left in North America with jaguars is Mexico. They come to Belize to hunt because there are more jaguars, and then they just drive the skin across the Mexican border."

The thought of jaguars being shot to complete some sort of check-list was sickening. I asked Darryl what he thought would stop or at least decrease this type of hunting. He said that he, and most of the reputable hunting organizations he knew, were now refusing even to discuss the possibility of taking people out on hunts, but he said that less-reputable organizations often did. The only good news was that, because there were now fewer jaguars, and because these organizations usually had less-effective guides, even after paying for the hunt the hunter would often go home empty-handed.

Darryl remembered when jaguars had been so common that he was able to guarantee a kill on a hunt. He told me that he would sometimes find a jaguar by looking for blood under trees. He had seen several jaguars eating full-grown cows that they had dragged up into trees. Darryl also said that it was not uncommon for jaguars to kill the dogs that were trying to tree them.

I had had enough of hunting stories so I told Darryl that I was worried about snakes. He said that was normal and was surprised that I didn't have a snake-bite kit. I had been told that because fer de lance have longer fangs than most snakes, the snake-bite kit would not be able to extract the venom. Darryl said he had a new snake-bite kit that used extremely powerful suction, and he thought it would work even on fer de lance bites. He gave me the kit and told me to be careful. At least it was a lot easier to use than antivenin.

With all the advice and warnings I had received since I arrived in Belize, I was now better prepared and more eager to get back to the jaguars in the Cockscomb.

# 5

# LIFE IN THE BUSH

**B**ack in the Cockscomb, I found some scats and more tracks. I was learning more about tracking as I went along, but progress was slow because I couldn't confirm my guesses. Besides tracks, I also found a few scrapes, the markings a jaguar makes on the ground by pulling its two front paws in toward its body. Usually there is a small pile of debris left at the end of the scrape. I had read that most scrapes have droppings on them, but most of the ones I found did not.

While out on the trails looking for tracks or driving in my Rover, I often saw wildlife I had only read about. Once when I was driving back to the Cockscomb after visiting a nearby village I saw what at first looked like a monkey run across the road in front of me. I stopped the Rover and a second animal crossed the road, then a third, and I realized they weren't monkeys at all but rather coatimundi. They are often called just "coatis" and the Creole name for them is "quash." I watched two more coatis cross the road in front of the Rover and waited for more, but this was a small group of just five animals.

They looked to me like a cross between a monkey and a raccoon, with their long banded tails and pointed muzzles. The tail, which is used for balancing while they feed in trees, is held upright, like a monkey's, when they travel on the ground. Coatis often travel in bands of females and young males; these groups sometimes are made up of as many as 20 animals.

Though I had been finding lots of paca hair in the jaguar droppings, I had been living in the Cockscomb for several weeks before I saw my first wild paca. One evening, just after dark, I had driven around one of the bends in the road, heading in to Quam Bank, when my headlights lit up a pair of eyes on the road ahead of me. The animal scurried across the road and disappeared into the bush on the other side.

I had seen a paca once before, at Maya Centre, but it had been captured along with its young and was in a cage. Ignacio had been out gathering one of his crops when he saw a female paca and her young standing perfectly still near his feet. He reached down and threw the mother, then the baby, into his sack and took them home to fatten up. His children had grown fond of the duo so he kept them as pets for a while.

Pacas are large rodents and can weigh up to 22 pounds (10 kg). They aren't as large as their relatives, the capybaras, but an adult paca would make a sizeable meal for a jaguar. The large head and body of the paca is offset by small legs and a short tail. The paca's coat looks remarkably similar to that of a spotted deer fawn.

Unfortunately for pacas, they taste good, and not just to jaguars. Paca is one of the delicacies in Belize and was even served to Queen Elizabeth when she visited here. The fact that the paca is a rodent obviously disturbed some news people, because the headline "She Ate A Rat!" appeared in several tabloids when the Queen returned to Britain. The large number of jaguar scats with paca bones in them suggested that the jaguars were enjoying the paca too.

Almost every day I found some evidence of jaguars, but often it was just a trace. Many of the bridges past Quam Bank had recently caved in and the back road could no longer be used by vehicles. It amazed me how quickly the dirt road became overgrown, engulfed by the jungle. Almost immediately much of the road became covered with grass, making it difficult to find tracks. Most of the scats I found had no tracks near them. I was finding more scats than I had thought I would, so at least I was able to gather information about jaguars' diets and their intestinal parasites. Parasites could be determined only from samples that were found fresh and then quickly preserved.

Diet could be determined from any sample, regardless of its age. If the dropping was fresh, I would scoop off part to be preserved for parasite analysis and then sun-dry the rest. Jaguar scats often contained large pieces of bone and clumps of hair from the prey animal. The bones would later be compared to a bone collection at the Royal Ontario Museum by vertebrate-paleontologist Kevin Seymour to determine the species of prey.

Sometimes the prey species were obvious, even to me. In one scat, I found several river-turtle heads and feet that were easily identifiable, and in another I found a large anteater claw. It was amazing that these sharp bones didn't puncture the big cats' intestines, but each bone appeared to be wrapped in a ball of the prey's fur.

I had just come back from the trail when Nari came running toward me, yelling "Miss Melanie!" in a rather desperate way. He had hired Gregorio to help take a zinc roof off a building. While on the roof, Gregorio had slipped and fallen about 15 feet (4.5 m). As he had come down, he had hit the edge of a truck and had injured his back. Nari had dragged him into a cabin, assuring him he was okay, and it had taken half an hour for Nari to realize that Gregorio was in a very bad state. We thought his back might have been broken, but we knew no ambulance would come back here. Luckily, three Americans had just driven in with a pick-up truck. I got a foam mattress and we carefully put him in the back of the truck.

As we were leaving, Nari came up and told me he couldn't go with us. I don't remember what reason he gave, but I do remember it was a stupid one. He handed me enough money to cover gas for both vehicles and said he would pay me later for any further expenses. I think he'd forgotten whose fault it was that Gregorio had been up on the roof by himself.

Al, one of the Americans, came with me in the Rover and we drove behind the slow-moving truck along the 6-mile (10-km) road to the highway. I could see that Gregorio was being bounced around in the back of the truck even though one of the American men was trying to hold him steady. We followed behind the pick-up in the Land Rover until we got to Maya Centre, where I stopped to get Gregorio's wife. It seemed to take her a long time to get ready. Then she appeared with her ten-month-old baby and eight-year-old son, and got into the Land Rover leaving the other five kids at home.

I caught up with the truck after 15 miles (24 km). The driver had just stopped to give Gregorio a chance to recover from the bouncing movement of the truck. His wife jumped out of my car and rushed over to Gregorio. She grabbed his hand and started to lament in Mayan. Gregorio, who was floating in and out of consciousness, tried to talk, but mostly he just moaned.

Two hours later when we arrived at Dangriga Hospital, they had to call for the doctor, who wasn't on the premises. Although there were four nurses standing nearby, we were asked to lift Gregorio onto the stretcher and then to transfer him onto a bed inside. The Americans, to whom I was grateful for helping, had to leave then, and 20 minutes later the doctor arrived. He walked up to Gregorio, banged him on the chest, and asked him what was wrong. I couldn't believe it! Gregorio had managed to gasp to a nurse that his chest and lower back were the problem, but she obviously hadn't told the doctor, so I did. The doctor then twisted Gregorio's legs until Gregorio yelled out, whereupon he told Gregorio to stop acting like a woman. Then he turned to me and apologized for the comment.

He discovered that Gregorio could not move his left leg and suggested that the problem might be a fractured tailbone. Since the X-ray machine was broken, he suggested we send Gregorio up to Belize City Hospital by ambulance. That trip would involve over 100 miles (160 km) of the worst road in the country. I asked if such a journey might not cause further damage, and the doctor replied that it might, but that the ambulance was the only form of transportation he had available.

I suggested sending Gregorio by plane. The doctor agreed that that would be much better, but informed me that I would have to pay for it myself. I called the airline and they said it would cost 250 Belize dollars. I knew I wouldn't get another cent from Nari, but it would be too cruel to send Gregorio up by road. I just hoped that there was enough money left in my account to cover the cheque.

Twenty minutes later we were putting Gregorio on the plane. His wife and baby were going along too. Gregorio regained consciousness just as we were about to shut the door and said he wouldn't go by plane. He tried to roll off the stretcher, which upset his wife. When I approached the stretcher and asked him why, he mumbled that he didn't have the money to take a plane. I said it was okay, that Nari had said he would pay for it. Gregorio still didn't want to go by plane; he was certain that Nari would never pay me back. The situation was getting ridiculous. Nari grew more annoying by the minute, and he wasn't even here. After I assured Gregorio and his wife that they would not have to pay for the flight, they left for Belize City.

I was starting to feel a bit worn out, and I just wanted to get back to the Cockscomb. As usual I was starving, so I took Gregorio's young son to a restaurant and found out he was as hungry as I was. Even though he was undoubtedly worried that his mother and father had disappeared into an airplane, he was being a good sport about it, and was quite excited about eating in a restaurant.

By the time I got back to my cabin in the Cockscomb, I was exhausted. Ignacio had told me at the gate that Nari was gone and wouldn't be back for at least a week. When he did come back, he quickly packed his bags and left, telling Ignacio he would come by later with the money for me. I never saw Nari again. Luckily Gregorio had only severely bruised his spine and recovered completely within the year.

My daily schedule in the Cockscomb was far different from what it had been at home. Most nights I would go to bed before nine and then be up by five the next morning. Much of the day was spent doing chores that would have taken only minutes at home. For example, water had to be carried up from the creek almost every day.

One task that I really disliked was doing the laundry. Mom used to keep an old scrub board in the basement of our house and I had always thought of it as an interesting antique, not as a useful tool. Now I used a scrub board and a bucket to do my laundry. I was forever scrubbing the skin off my knuckles, and the first clothes I washed always looked best because I would run out of energy by the end. I couldn't imagine having an entire family's laundry to do this way. Sheets were the worst, because they were so awkward. Drying them was another problem. As it was the rainy season it was important to do my laundry on a day when there were at least a few hours of sunshine. Sometimes I would guess wrong and my clothes and sheets would stay wet for days.

At noon I would go down to the creek to bathe. One nice thing about the Cockscomb is that there isn't anything dangerous in the water. The first time I had gone into the creek to wash up, I had felt something bite my leg. I stumbled out of the water and then felt rather foolish when I found out that the tiny fish in the water feel a lot worse than they look. After that I got used to them nipping at my legs every day.

My first morning activity was to go out looking for tracks. It would rain often, but not usually first thing in the morning. It was important to get out before the tracks and scat were washed away. In other ways the rain was quite helpful. It made the soil better for tracking and it meant I didn't have to spend so much time lugging water up from the creek. If it didn't rain, it would usually be too hot to be very active by about 11:00 a.m. and that's when I would bathe in the river, and wash clothes if necessary. When it cooled down a little in the mid to late afternoon, I would go out on a different trail from the one I had taken in the morning and continue to search for tracks and scat. All scat had to be dried in the sun and then bagged and labelled. I also kept a journal, which I wrote in either in the early afternoon or after dark by lamplight.

I went to Dangriga for mail only about once a week since the trip was time-consuming and gas was so expensive. It was great to get mail from home, so I made sure I wrote all of my friends in order to keep the mail coming. Some of my letters became pages in my journal and vice versa. As I read about exams and apartments and television, it felt like I was a world away. Sometimes I would get a bout of homesickness after reading a letter, and would wish I could see or even just talk to my family and friends. Though I had lived alone in Toronto for several years, I could always pick up the telephone, or hop on the subway to visit someone, whenever I felt lonely. Now I was learning to appreciate the luxury of being able to turn on the television or the radio when I wanted to hear a human voice. Batteries were precious and so I rarely used my radio while I was in the Cockscomb.

I also missed the cycling exercise. Though I walked quite a bit every day, it was nothing like the intense training I had been doing to prepare for the bike race. I had never enjoyed running, so to keep in shape I used food cans as weights and a rope to skip with. Sometimes, while I was bathing, I would tread water in the deeper part of the creek.

It was hard to keep track of time in the Cockscomb because it never really mattered what day it was. Luckily I had bought a digital watch that told me the date and the day of the week, otherwise I would never have been able to keep track. One day I drove all the way to Dangriga to get my mail, only to find that the post office was closed. I was peering through the glass door at the dark interior when someone walked by and told me that the post office was always closed on Saturdays. I had been aware of the schedule, but not of what day it was.

For me, the advantages of living in the Cockscomb far outweighed the inconveniences. The bathing creek was beautiful and much nicer than the shower stall I had at home. At night, instead of traffic, I would hear frogs chorusing loudly, and during the day a kiskadee flycatcher, a beautiful, bright yellow bird, would fly up and land on the tree by my cabin door. This was the first September in 18 years that I had not been sitting in a school classroom, and I would learn more this year than I had in any of those previous ones.

It was one month since I had arrived and picked out my cabin in the Cockscomb. Renee would be coming to visit soon and every time I called or wrote home I asked my parents to send down more things with Renee. My list was quite varied and included such things as camping plates and utensils, waterproof matches, extra sheets, batteries, Kool-aid, and – most important of all – maple syrup.

Several days later I drove up to Belize City to meet Renee. When she arrived, I found that Mom and Dad had sent down a wonderful Care package containing even more than I had asked for. At my favourite camp store, they had bought a shower bag to hang in the sun and then get a warm shower under. Grant, the store manager, knew me, so he sent down some fun samples for me to try, including a tiny bottle of oil of eucalyptus that was supposed to work on everything from aching muscles to insect bites. They also sent dishes, an old pair of drapes so I wouldn't have to change in the dark, a water bag with a spout on it, and even some home-made cookies. Renee had brought me a Trivial Pursuit game with which to while away the evening hours.

After I picked Renee up at the airport, I drove her around Belize City to show her the sights. We drove past the swing bridge, located in the middle of town; a group of my friends were busily painting it bright green. They were part of the Leos, a young Lions Club, and were working on projects to improve the city.

Winston, whom I had met through some other friends who worked at the Fort George Hotel, joked that if we helped paint the bridge it would give Renee a chance to "meet the locals." It was a hot day and they looked miserable, but brightened up when we offered to help. We put on our grubbies and spent most of the day on the bridge. I was glad I had changed since I had more bright green paint on me than on the bridge railings. Perhaps it would help me blend in in the bush. Cars and motorcycles honked as they passed over the bridge, and drivers cheered us on or commented on the brightness of the paint.

We finally finished and the firemen from the fire station nearby invited us all to drop by to try to get the paint off us. When we were less spotted, we all went home to shower and change and then met again to go out dancing. Renee and I didn't stay long because I was fighting a cold and my stomach wasn't doing so well either. I was worse the next day, but we headed down to the Cockscomb anyway.

As soon as we got to Quam Bank, we had to bathe in the creek to get the dust off ourselves. I explained to her about the nipping fish so she wouldn't be as startled by them as I had been. She bathed among the fish with great humour. Renee was a fun person, but she could be practical when she had to be. Though she had never been out of Ontario before, she was a great sport about everything and would often amaze me with her ability to adapt to the different circumstances in Belize. As she was also eight inches taller than me and quite strong, she was a great help with the heavier work that I had trouble doing on my own.

By the time we got back to the cabin it was almost dark. It was nice to have someone to talk to again, and Renee and I stayed up late, catching up on everything. It was good to hear about everyone from home and about my friends at the university. I told Renee how much I was enjoying the Cockscomb, about all the exotic wildlife I had seen and how I hoped I would soon see my first wild jaguar. Then I told her that sometimes, when I was in Quam Bank alone and went out on a trail, I would wonder what would happen if I got bitten by a snake, or just tripped and broke an ankle. The thought of being badly hurt and not being able to get help scared me, but now that Renee was here the fear was alleviated.

I had spent the last few nights I was in the Cockscomb making stakes out of dead wood to use as distance markers and spray-painting the tops bright orange. Renee and I spent much of the next week pacing off all the main trails and putting in a stake every 650 feet (200 m). On each stake I wrote the distance from the beginning of the trail. This system would help me record more accurately the locations of the tracks and scat I found. It would also help me find tracks and scat reported by Ignacio or Pedro.

Several days after Renee arrived, Ignacio told us that two nights earlier two jaguars had been seen courting near Maya Centre. Renee and I headed out to Maya Centre and tried to find the man who had told Ignacio about them. We were planning to spend the night in the Land Rover, waiting to see if the jaguars came back. We were one day too late. A hunter had heard about the two jaguars and had shot the male the next night, when the jaguars returned. The hunter was not local, but was from farther south, so we decided to travel down the highway to the next major village to see if we could gather any more information there.

We couldn't seem to find out anything more about the kill, so we headed back toward Maya Centre. Whoever had killed that jaguar may not have realized that it was now illegal to shoot them. If the hunter didn't know, I wanted to tell him; if he did know, or if he was involved in the illegal fur trade, then I would report him.

We stopped at a hut on the side of the road that had a 7-Up sign hanging on it. I asked the store owner if he knew anything about a jaguar that had been killed the previous night. He panicked, telling me he was sorry, that he hadn't meant to kill the jaguar, but he'd been afraid it would hurt him. He said he had been out hunting and had killed a paca to bring home for dinner when a jaguar had appeared in front of him on the trail. Fearing that the cat would attack him to get at the raw meat, he shot it. I asked him what he had done with it and he offered to show us.

Renee and I followed him from the hut into the bush, along a narrow footpath. He was walking quickly and it was difficult to keep up. I thought he had taken us out to lose us, so I ran ahead, into a clearing. There, I found the shop owner standing beside a jaguar skull that he had hung on a tree branch to be cleaned of flesh. Flies covered it and it smelled foul. He said he had kept the skull in case he could sell it, or the teeth. Then he offered to sell it to me.

On the one hand, I was angry; on the other, I couldn't really blame this man for shooting the cat in the circumstances he had described. It must have been quite frightening to confront a 150-pound (68-kg) cat, while carrying a freshly killed paca. I told him that jaguars were disappearing and that he should never shoot another one. He said he had never shot one before, and hoped he never saw one again while he was hunting.

He led us to the front of another thatched hut where a beautiful jaguar skin was stretched out on wooden poles, drying in the sun. I asked him how the skull had gotten so clean overnight and was shocked to find out he had killed this cat two nights earlier. Obviously this was a different jaguar from the one that had been killed while courting. It was a depressing thought: two jaguars had been killed in the same area and on two consecutive nights.

The store owner hadn't told anyone other than his son that he had killed the jaguar and the fact that I knew about it made him nervous. I didn't let on that I had been looking for another cat. There was a chance that he would spread the word that we would somehow know when people killed jaguars.

A rancher near Maya Centre had said I could borrow a horse if I needed one for tracking. I thought a horse would be helpful on the back trails, and it would mean I could carry more camera and field equipment with me. I had arranged to go see about the horse the next day.

It rained heavily all that night and we left early, just in case the road to Maya Centre was really bad. It was muddy, but I was getting better at not getting stuck, and I rarely needed the four-wheel drive anymore. I picked up speed going around a corner on the road, and then had to slam on the brakes. We had come to an impasse. Though it was broad daylight I couldn't see the road. In every direction was thick green jungle. We got out of the Rover and discovered that a huge tree had fallen across the road, dragging hundreds of vines with it. The mass was so dense we couldn't see the road on the other side.

I decided that the Land Rover could push through a spot where there were only vines and small branches. I slowly edged forward and heard loud crunching noises that sounded promising. I backed up to try again and felt something dragging my left tire. The vines were stronger than I had thought. They had broken one front light and crushed the front corner of the Rover into the tire. We kicked the dent out far enough that the metal didn't rub the tire and decided to try a different strategy. Renee and I got out our machetes and started cutting. After developing a few blisters, we finally managed to cut a hole big enough to get the vehicle through.

I felt as though we were running an obstacle course that day. We then had to cross a creek that had been flooded by the rain. Normally the water level reached only half-way up the Rover's tires. But when we got to the creek it looked really high. We decided we weren't going to turn back now. I backed the Rover up and took a run for it and was glad I did. The water was higher than the bottom of the doors, but we took on only a little water.

When we finally got to the rancher's, he said I wouldn't be able to get a horse for another six weeks; Queen Elizabeth would be visiting Belize soon and his horses were needed for the parade.

By the time we returned to the cabin, I was exhausted. I hadn't been able to get rid of my cold or my intestinal problems and I was starting to lose weight. Renee said it looked as though I had lost about 15 pounds (7 kg) since she had arrived, and the previous night I had started vomiting. I was drinking a lot of fluids, but I was feeling very weak. It was time to see a doctor in Dangriga.

After a short rest, we got into the car but, to our dismay, it wouldn't start. I looked under the hood to see what the trouble was and decided to top up the oil, which I noticed was low. I grabbed a screwdriver to puncture a hole in the can. But in my haste to fix the car, I hadn't propped the hood up properly and my banging brought the hood slamming down onto my hand. The entire fingerprint area of my index finger was sliced off and hanging by a single strip of skin. My middle finger hurt even more and was bleeding so heavily it was hard to determine the extent of the injury. Both fingers were also covered in oil, because I had just managed to puncture the can before the hood had fallen.

Renee ran inside to get some water to wash my hand. While she was inside I started to feel sorry for myself. The hood had just missed my head by inches. I kept thinking about what would have happened if I had been leaning forward just a bit farther when the hood had come down. Now it was even more important that I get to a doctor, but I couldn't fix the car with my hand bleeding so heavily. I was worried that I wouldn't be able to get my hand stitched back together and that I might lose the two fingertips. Meanwhile, the diarrhea and nausea were getting worse and I was starting to panic. If Renee hadn't been there, I probably would have just collapsed into a heap and given up.

After most of the oil had been rinsed off my hand, I stuck the severed portion of my fingers back on as well as I could. I remembered what a friend of mine had told me: if you can't stitch skin in place, just stick it back together as well as you can and it might hold. I had raised my hand above my heart to stop the bleeding, but the throbbing was severe.

In the cabin, I lay down, with my arm up; then Renee and I started kidding around about our "attack" Rover. My hand didn't hurt as much when I didn't think about it, so Renee and I played Trivial Pursuit all evening. Renee made rice with cheese sauce, which she thought tasted awful, but I was so hungry I thought it was great. I was sick after dinner again, then fell asleep with my arm propped up on pillows; but every few hours it would slip and the throbbing would start again. I knew I had to fix the car the next day so I could get to a doctor.

Finally it was morning and I went out to see if I could get the car going. I made sure I propped the hood open properly this time. I fiddled a bit under the hood and tried to start it up. Suddenly the engine turned over and caught! I was afraid to turn it off, so Renee grabbed everything we needed for town and we drove off.

When I got to the doctor he suggested we remove the flaps of skin I had so carefully aligned; he was concerned about infection. He said it was too late to stitch the skin back in place, but I disagreed and decided to leave the flaps where they were and to be really careful about keeping the wound clean. The two fingers did eventually heal and the scars are barely noticeable today.

By that time I was more worried about my intestinal problems since I was feeling worse by the minute. I had to excuse myself to run to the bathroom several times during my conversation with the doctor. He told me that it would be difficult to determine what was wrong with me because he had limited testing facilities. He gave me several prescriptions; I was to take them sequentially, replacing each one that failed to work with the next. He also gave me an injection to decrease the nausea, at least until we got back to the Cockscomb.

Renee offered to drive, and we stopped to pick up my mail at the post office. There was a large package for me from the United States. It was from Al, one of the Americans who had helped me after Gregorio's accident. He was planning to set up a business in Belize and had sent me a Coleman kerosene lantern to use until he got there. He said I could use it for as long as I needed it and then drop it off for him. We bought a pop bottle full of kerosene for 25 cents and I tried not to spill it all over myself on the bumps in the road.

When we got back, I fell asleep and Renee went out on the trail. She didn't find any tracks, but she did come across a small fer de lance on her way back to the cabin. She had managed to get by it without disturbing it, and seemed to be enjoying herself. I was glad she was such a good sport about everything, but I felt bad that I was so sick during her visit.

It was getting dark, so we decided to try the new lantern. It lit up the whole cabin. After using hurricane lanterns and candles for light, it was like having electricity again. I felt as though this was the best present I had ever received. Now I had three more hours in every day. We opened up a can of bacon to celebrate. (We were getting sick of rice and beans and eggs.) It smelled great cooking, but we both spit out our first bite. The bacon was preserved in salt, which I hadn't known, and was inedible. I couldn't bring myself to throw it out, so we boiled it, which helped a little. Next time I would know to wash the salt off first. To avoid dehydration, which the doctor had told me was the worst aspect of diarrhea, I was drinking a lot of water. However, I was afraid that I had picked up the bug by drinking untreated river water, so now I was boiling everything. I was still losing weight and feeling weak all the time.

Renee and I sat up playing Trivial Pursuit and enjoying the lantern. After a while we had to stop because we couldn't hear ourselves above the frog chorus outside the cabin. We were yelling as loudly as we could, but the frogs were obviously in the middle of mating season and the noise was deafening.

Later, when we went to bed, we heard a strange thumping noise in the corner of the cabin, in the main room, where Renee was sleeping. We got out the flashlight and shone it into the corner. There, on the top of a 7-Up bottle, a female frog was crouched precariously on the edge, laying her eggs in the empty bottle. We picked her up and put her outside, where, one hoped, her efforts would meet with better success.

The next morning I heard a yelp from the other room and the sound of Renee leaping out of her bed. "What's long and black and has a long tail and lots of legs?" she asked. "A scorpion," I replied. "Oh yuk, one just fell off the ceiling and landed on my face and then fell on the floor." I was worried that she had been stung, but obviously the scorpion had seen her as a landing-spot and not as a threat.

I had been stung by a scorpion once while I was picking up firewood so I knew how painful such a sting could be. I had kicked the log first as a precaution and nothing seemed to be on it. I wasn't sure what had stung my finger at first, so I carefully lifted the log and found a scorpion flattened against it. I quickly cut off the circulation in my finger and sucked out the cut. I was quite proud of my first-aid efforts when I didn't get sick, but later I discovered that the scorpions in the Cockscomb weren't dangerously poisonous.

That day we decided to drive the Rover for the first mile and a quarter (2 km) and then track back from that position since the first part of the back logging road was getting overgrown with grass. I had avoided taking the Rover back there because the bridge was falling apart and, this time, it creaked and groaned so much I decided this would be my last drive over it. That morning I had decided to try a liquid diet for a few days. If nothing else it would prevent dehydration. But the liquid diet was not helping, and once we started walking,

I had to run into the bushes every mile or so. It was getting hot, so we stopped at one of the creeks and waded in to cool off. We had run out of water and had to drink from the creek. However, since Renee had been drinking creek water since her arrival, I was beginning to think that my illness had been caused by something else.

We found and measured some jaguar tracks farther along the trail, and then headed back the way we had come. We were covering ground more quickly now because we were retracing our steps and didn't have to search intently for tracks. Suddenly I noticed a whole row of fresh tracks heading the same way we had gone out. The jaguar had obviously been following us! The tracks ended on a grassy section and it was impossible to tell how much farther it had followed us. I measured the tracks while Renee kept watch for the jaguar. It was a bit disconcerting, so I just kept repeating to Renee that jaguars don't attack people.

There were lots of tracks and there was no shelter against the sun where I was measuring. I had felt awful on awakening that morning, and now Renee was feeling sick too. We had been out in the sun a long time and, finally, I couldn't take it any more, and just rolled over and lay on my back on the trail. Renee laughed until she realized that I was not planning to get up. I kept saying that I just wanted to sleep for a bit. She tried to get me to move into the shade, but I wouldn't. Finally, she dragged me to my feet, and we both barely managed to get back to the car.

There were tracks near the car too, and I measured them while Renee dozed in the car. Every 15 minutes I had to take a break and sit with her in the Rover. It wasn't any cooler in there but at least it offered cover from the sun and a place to sit. When I had finished measuring, we drove back to the cabin and drank what seemed like gallons of water.

I collapsed when we got back and Renee commented that if I had been alone that afternoon I would probably still be lying in the middle of the trail, in the sun. I'd been sick for almost four full weeks, and I had been in Belize only two months. There was no point in my staying in the Cockscomb in this shape. I realized then that I had to go back to Canada as soon as I could and see a tropical-disease specialist. It was frustrating to think that I had come this far, only to leave, but I knew that in Toronto I would at least be able to be tested thoroughly and be prescribed the right medication. I hoped to be back in Belize within a week or two.

The next morning, I decided I might as well eat solids again, because abstaining from them hadn't made any difference. I felt a bit better and went on with my work. Out on the trail, we found two sets of tracks. It looked like one cat walking along the trail and another walking in the opposite direction. It could have been the same animal but, since the tracks coming back were a bit smaller, that was unlikely. We hadn't been able to find any scat, and when it started to rain, we gave up the search and headed back to the cabin for lunch.

Later that day I decided to try my trip-mechanism camera set-up. There were very few photographs of jaguars in the wild and I hoped that the trip mechanisms would allow me to get some without disturbing the jaguars. Pictures would confirm without any doubt that the animals I was tracking were jaguars and not cougars, and if I got lucky, they might enable me to distinguish individual cats.

One of my customers at the bicycle shop back in Toronto was Geoff Salter, an electronic whiz. When I told him I needed a mechanism to attach to my cameras that could be activated by a passing animal, Geoff designed a camera trip mechanism, using an infra-red-beam garage-door opener. All the animal had to do was to break the infra-red beam by walking between the beam producer and a reflector that was placed yards away to automatically set off the camera. In case that didn't work, Geoff also designed a pressure plate made from a geometry set box, elastic bands and a sponge. Placed under something, a piece of wood, for example, it would activate the camera when anything exerted pressure on it.

I had read that jaguars were sensitive to catnip, so I decided it would make an inexpensive bait for my pressure plates. The trip-mechanisms had all worked perfectly at home, but I wasn't sure if they would work in the tropical weather. Some of my other equipment was shorting out and breaking down in the humidity.

Renee and I set up the equipment about a mile and a quarter (2 km) from the cabin, on the main back trail. I hammered the infra-red-beam device into the ground on one side of the trail and stuck in the bicycle reflector across from it, mounted on a stick. The cameras were set up on opposite sides so that I could get a front and rear shot of anything that walked along the trail. We hadn't brought our flashlights along because it had been long before dusk when we'd left. Now we had to walk back to the cabin in the dark.

The next day I felt a bit stronger and Renee was completely over whatever she had had. We went back to check the camera set-up. It had rained during the night, but luckily we had covered both cameras and the infra-red device with plastic. There were no tracks to be seen, but the rain might have washed them away. When I walked through the beam, nothing happened. I tried again, but no cameras flashed. All that work, for nothing. We took the set-up apart and carried everything back to the cabin.

The problem seemed to be in the infra-red device and not in the camera or the connecting wires. It had worked well when I'd tried it in Toronto, but with the high humidity and all the rain in the Cockscomb, I shouldn't have been surprised that it didn't function here.

I decided to try the pressure plate with the cameras, but this time using the main road. That way we could drive all the equipment to the site and use the car headlights if it got dark. I used a large, flat board I had found in camp to set on top of the pressure plate. It was difficult to set it to trigger with just the right amount of weight. I didn't want it to be set off by the rain.

Again it got dark quickly and then it started to rain. Suddenly, I heard something in the bush behind me. After Renee talked me out of the Rover and told me that I couldn't possibly know it was a jaguar, I was still nervous. When I dumped the catnip on the pressure plate I slipped and set the cameras off. The flash startled me (I was already jumpy), and I now have a photo of myself wide-eyed with catnip on my hands.

We had just started off in the Rover again when Renee said that she wished she could see one large mammal before she left. Seconds later we saw a jaguar on the road ahead. It was an exhilarating experience. Its eyes blazed yellow out of the darkness. It was a big cat, and I hadn't really understood how powerful jaguars could be until this moment. The body was very large in proportion to the legs.

The cat crouched low and stared back fearlessly. Then, it turned its back and walked away from us, down the dirt road, the car headlights focused on it as if it were on a stage. I put my foot heavily on the gas pedal, afraid we would lose sight of the jaguar, and it looked back over its shoulder and crouched in a strange manner. I would later see a zoo jaguar crouch that way and spray urine backwards, but it was too dark that night to see more than the crouch.

The jaguar lumbered along the road until I moved the Rover too close, and then it stepped to one side and looked back at us, as if to let us pass. I braked and waited, and with a look of what I can only describe as annoyance, it walked right back into the middle of the road and continued on its way. I was madly trying to get my camera ready and to drive at the same time. My hands were shaking with excitement and suddenly the old familiar camera equipment seemed horribly complicated. I moved in closer to get a picture, but once again the powerful feline stepped off the road and into the bushes. This time I thought it was gone, but as we inched forward I caught a glimpse of its gold-and-black fur.

We waited in the darkness, hoping it would come back, and finally it strolled back into the centre of the road. This time it turned and faced us, and I was hypnotized by its piercing eyes. I remembered how it could break a capybara's head open like a nutshell and I felt vulnerable behind the thin windshield. It stared for a moment and then, once again, it turned its back, as if we weren't worth considering any longer, and walked away down the road. When I gained control of myself again, I sped toward it and leaned out the window to take a picture. As the flash went off, its muscles tensed and it sprang into the bushes. I thought at the time that the cat was too far away for the flash to capture it and I had been right: the picture didn't turn out. We waited a long time in the darkness but the cat didn't return within sight of the car.

That night, back in the cabin, we were both reading, but we kept saying, "Wasn't that incredible?" and "Do you believe it?" every few minutes. Now I really wanted to stay in the Cockscomb rather than go back to Canada, but I knew I was too sick.

I had promised to take Renee to Guatemala before she left for home. I really didn't feel well enough to go, but I didn't think it would be fair to cancel now. We drove up to Belize City and planned to leave for

Guatemala the next day. In the meantime, I tried to find Vincent. I wanted to learn more about the jungle and about tracking, and I had asked several cyclists if any of them could come down to the Cockscomb for a few days and teach me about tracking. No one wanted to go into the bush at all, and they said they didn't know anything about tracking or the bush. But they told me that Vincent was one of the best trackers around.

Vincent was also one of the finest cyclists in Belize. He was a strong, rugged-looking Creole man in his late 20s who had spent much of his life in the bush. I had never met him before, but I decided to talk to him about tracking. I found him at the Church Street corner, where all the cyclists hang out. I knew there had just been a bicycle race in Belize City so I asked him how he had done. He said that he hadn't participated because he'd been "back a bush" all weekend. When I asked him what he had been doing back in the bush, he said he was just spending some time. I knew I had found myself a tracker.

I told him I was going home to Toronto for a week or two to get better, but that I could use his help when I came back. When Renee, who had been looking around town, came by to join us, we mentioned our trip to Guatemala and asked Vincent if he knew anyone who spoke Spanish who might want to come along. I was surprised when he said that he did, since few Creoles speak Spanish. We arranged to pick him up the next morning, and headed back to the guest house.

It was several hours of driving, so we headed off first thing the next morning. The Belize/Guatemala border was only an hour and a half by car from Belize City. Just before we reached the border, I noticed a path on the other side of the river, leading into the bush. It was a very well-worn path and several women, carrying baskets, were taking it. Vincent said that the local people would often shop in Guatemala and used that trail to go around the border station.

I had been to the Maya ruins in Tikal, Guatemala, before, but things had obviously deteriorated since my last trip. The first army check-point was the same as usual, with young boys holding machine guns and examining passports. We were stopped at several new check-points along the highway and were further delayed by a group of machine-gun-carrying guerrillas standing by an empty bus. They wore the same uniforms as army soldiers, but Vincent told us that army soldiers always did up their shirts to the collar. These boys wore unbuttoned shirts and bandannas. We pretended we didn't understand them by saying "Touristo, touristo" and waving our passports in the air. Vincent spoke Spanish quite well, but because he was Creole they didn't think he did. They finally let us go and we drove the last 2 miles (3 km) to Tikal. At the entrance, we saw several tourists lugging their suitcases through the main gate and we stopped to give them a lift.

A tired-looking Englishman jumped into our Land Rover with his suitcase and said he wished we had come two hours earlier. He had been on the bus when the guerrillas leapt out of the bush, stopped the bus and made the passengers get out and walk to Tikal.

Renee and Vincent went out to see the ruins and I slept the rest of the day. The next day I went out to get a picture of the Temple of the Jaguar, a huge construction with narrow steps to the top. We climbed to the top of another ruin that was above the jungle canopy. From it we could see for miles, to other ruins swallowed up by the jungle. I had seen excavation sights in Belize, and they had looked like small mounds of dirt in the bush before excavation. It was an eerie experience to look down on these huge, ancient monuments that were still much as they must have been when Tikal had been a bustling Mayan community. This was not a place for anyone who was leery of heights. There was no barrier to protect the clumsy from falling hundreds of feet to their deaths below. Vultures were landing noisily on the monument ledge above our heads, and I wondered if I looked as shaky as I felt.

We stood in silence for several minutes and then suddenly I heard a most horrifying noise – a roar that belonged on the soundtrack of a monster movie. It seemed to be coming from all around us, up from the jungle below. It increased in intensity and then stopped, its echo lingering only a moment. "What was that?" I asked Vincent in an inexplicable whisper. "Howler monkeys," he replied. It was hard to believe that all that noise had come from a troop of monkeys. We could see dark shapes in the tree-tops off in the distance, so I guessed he was right. Howler monkeys are the largest on the continent, some growing to almost 3 feet (1 m) in height. They have thick prehensile tails, and huge lower jaws and throat areas designed to make the eerie howling calls that can be heard up to 3 miles (5 km) away.

We headed back toward Belize City that afternoon, but only got as far as the main gate of the park before we were stopped, this time by the park security guard. He was armed with a rifle and asked us pleasantly enough if we would take his two Mayan women friends to their village down the highway. We were pretty crowded already, with all our luggage and three people, so Vincent suggested they wait a few minutes for the bus that was following us. The guard walked away, and I thought he was going to open the gate so we could get out of the park. But he just stood there. Vincent laughed and called to him in Spanish. I asked him what he had said, because the two women were hurrying toward the Rover. He told me that there was no point in arguing with someone who had control over a gate and was carrying a rifle. We rearranged all the luggage and crammed three of us in the front, and then headed off.

The guerrillas were farther along the road this time and just around a corner. The brakes on the Rover were not very good, and I thought I was going to hit one of the armed men who jumped out in front of it. I was madly gearing down and they scrambled out of the way, but I could see them aiming their guns at the Rover through my rear-view mirror. I was pretty sure they wouldn't shoot, but wasn't about to take that chance. We pulled over, and they ran up to the car and asked us if we had seen any soldiers on the road so far. We hadn't, so they let us go.

A few miles farther down the road we were stopped at a new army check-point. They kept asking if we had seen anything, and Vincent kept saying no. They searched our luggage and wanted to take the Mayan women out of the car. The women were terrified, and Vincent murmured to me that they might be killed by the army if we left them there. The soldiers didn't seem to know what to do with us, because I kept saying no when they ordered the women out of the car.

Finally, they called over their superior and he turned out to be a Creole, originally from Belize. Vicent said that often, if Belizeans committed a crime, they would run to Guatemala. After several years, they could no longer be tried for the crime and they would return to Belize. Meanwhile, often they would have done quite well for themselves in Guatemala, which has a poorer quality of education than does Belize. Vincent knew the soldier's family and filled him in on what was going on in Belize, and he let us go on.

As we drove through the check-point area, we saw a truck full of Mayans – men, women and children. When our passengers saw them, they started to wail and tried to climb out of the back of the Rover. I asked Vincent if I should stop, but he said no or none of us would get out of there. Vincent went on to explain that often Mayans were stopped on the highway and if they had any guns with them they were in trouble. Since most lived off the land and carried rifles all the time, this was not uncommon. If any of the men on the truck had a rifle, he added, the soldiers might assume the whole truckload was supporting the guerrillas. Many Mayans "disappeared" in such encounters, he said finally.

Several miles down the road we came to a village and let the women off. I hadn't realized until then just how dangerous it was for the Mayans here. It was getting a bit too dangerous for us as well, and I looked forward to getting back to Belize. But before we returned, we were stopped again by the army. This time they told us to take six men with us down the road. There certainly wasn't enough room, but we didn't have a choice. They sat on the luggage and hung out the windows and each one banged on the side of the Rover when he wanted to be dropped off. The last one got out as we reached the border.

If I had known how dangerous the trip was to be, I wouldn't have gone to Guatemala in the first place. It was difficult to believe that two countries so close together could be so different. I understood now why the Mayans were smuggling themselves into Belize from Guatemala. It was good to be back on safe ground again.

The next day I took Renee to the airport and booked myself on the first available flight, which was two days later. I was feeling better that day, and decided not to waste it. I wanted to get a jaguar caller, like the ones some hunters used to mimic jaguar noises, to use when I got back to the Cockscomb. If hunters could use these callers to lure jaguars in to be shot, then I should be able to use one to call jaguars in to be photographed. I also wanted to record the jaguars' vocal response to the call. Several hunting books I had read said that jaguars often call back as they approach the calling hunter. Many hunters make callers out of a hollow gourd, with a goat skin stretched over the top. A waxed horse tail rope is pulled through a small hole in the goat skin and knotted at the top. The hunter then pulls the rope within the gourd and his fingers rub the wax, producing a sound similar to the jaguar's. The best callers, I had been told, were made out of hourglass-shaped gourds.

I would have to find the gourd first and then find someone who could make the caller. Vincent said he knew a man whose relatives had a farm north of Belize City where we would likely find the gourds I needed. When we went to pick up the man he asked if he could bring his wife and baby along for the ride. Soon the whole group of us were heading north. When we got to the farm, they told us that they didn't have such gourds, but they told us of another farm that might. We went to several farms, and each one told us the same thing. Finally, it was getting late and I decided to give up.

We were driving back to Belize City when I heard a scream from the back seat. The back door was open and the woman and her baby were gone. I pulled over immediately, but it took a moment for me to realize what had happened. We had been going around a corner at about 45 miles (72 km) an hour and the woman had leaned back against the door, with her elbow on the handle. We jumped out of the car and I ran to the baby. She was lying about 15 feet (5 m) from her mother. As I got to her, she started to cry and I was relieved that she was alive. But when I picked her up, I was shocked to see that one side of her head was covered with blood and was collapsed inward.

The mother looked even worse off. She was unconscious and through the large gash across her forehead I could see bone. Another car stopped to help and I yelled for them to get an ambulance. They told me that an ambulance wouldn't come all the way out here and suggested that we go to the British Army base near the airport, since there were good doctors there and it was 9 miles (14 km) closer to us than was Belize City.

The husband was in shock and said he couldn't lift his wife, even though she was not a large woman and he was a strong man. Vincent had two broken ribs from a recent fall, but he was obviously much better in an emergency. He scooped the woman up and laid her down in the back of the Rover. The husband kept saying that it was all his fault, that he had been leaning against his door and had motioned for his wife to lean on hers. His wife came to and started to scream for her baby, so Vincent showed her the side of the baby that was unhurt and she collapsed again.

We finally got to the army base and they took X-rays and examined the mother and baby and said they were well enough to go to Belize City Hospital. They said they would both be okay, and that they looked a lot worse than they were. We drove to Belize Hospital and they said the same thing. We waited in the hospital for most of the evening, then we all agreed to meet first thing in the morning. It wasn't very late, but I fell asleep as soon as I got back to my room. The next morning both mother and baby had improved and were out of danger.

Later that morning, I flew back to Toronto. I thought I would be returning to Belize within two weeks, but it would be two months before I was well enough to make the trip. I saw several tropical-disease specialists in Toronto and went through a battery of tests, but no one could figure out what was wrong with me. Everyone was amazed that I had avoided dehydration for so long. I was on a liquid diet for much of the two months I was home and I was too weak and sick to do anything except sleep.

It was frustrating not knowing how long this would last. One doctor said he thought it might be a permanent condition, so I suggested that I go back to Belize and be careful to drink fluids to avoid dehydration. But he said I was in no shape to go anywhere, and sent me back for more tests. Each time I felt a bit better, I would phone my friends in Belize City and tell them I thought I would be back the following week, but then I would get worse again.

I had been told to drink apple juice and consommé, and I was miserable. Normally, I love eating and indulge that passion. One day I ran out of apple juice and drank water. I soon realized that, for the first time in months, I wasn't getting extreme stomach cramps. Within two days my digestive tract was operating normally and I felt healthy again. I had another glass of apple juice and was sick for two days.

The doctors said that I had probably had some kind of infection, probably parasites, but one of the medicines I had been given in Belize had gotten rid of it. Because I had taken so much medicine, my stomach was much more sensitive and, in the meantime, I had obviously developed some kind of sensitivity to apple juice.

As soon as I was well again, I headed back to Belize. This time I was armed with a water filter. I wasn't sure there was a problem with the water in the Cockscomb but I was no longer willing to take that chance.

# 6

# TRACKING THE JAGUAR

For two months I had been writing to people in Belize to say that I would be back next week. When I finally did return, no one believed I was coming and so there was nobody to meet me at the airport. I saw one of the workers from the Fort George Hotel and he gave me a lift to the car-rental place. There, too, they had given up on me and had rented out my Rover. I wasn't thrilled with that since I was still paying for it. Instead, they gave me a temporary replacement with terrible brakes and loose steering. It was so bad that I took cabs around town to be safe.

It was good to be back in Belize again. For a while I had wondered if I'd ever get back. It was now mid-December, and the weather in Belize was sunny and warm – much nicer than the cold snowy Toronto weather. I dropped my luggage at the guest house and headed downtown. I wanted to get to the Cockscomb as soon as possible, but first I had to decide what to do about a vehicle. I had arranged to rent the Rover for only five months and now they wanted to double the rate because it was tourist season. I had arrived for this study on August 1 and had originally planned to leave in January; since I had missed two months, I would now stay until April.

I decided to buy a car, so I wouldn't be throwing my money away on rent. I walked to the downtown corner where all the cyclists hang out and announced that I was looking for a vehicle. Within 24 hours I had a list of all the vehicles that were for sale in Belize City. I needed four-wheel drive, and there weren't many available with that feature. I found one that was covered with fresh mud and figured that was a good sign. I asked Kenrick, an ex-cyclist who had won several Cross-Country races and his friend Don, who were both mechanics, if they could come and look over the truck for me. After we talked the owner down in price somewhat, I became the proud owner of my first truck.

I was getting ready to go back to the Cockscomb when Vincent dropped by and said he and his brother, Kurl, would come down to help me with the tracking. Vincent said he'd shop for groceries and share the cooking if I paid for the supplies.

Vincent led the way into a small shop (I had been going to the big grocery store). We bought paper bags full of flour, dried beans, honey in rum bottles, pigtails, and sweet potatoes. The only canned item we bought was condensed milk for coffee. We had bags and bags of food on the counter, but Vincent said they ate a lot. I was wondering if I would have to go back to the bank for more money, but the bill turned out to be incredibly low. It was less than half of what I usually paid for a week's supply of food and this pile was for three of us over five days. I now knew that the trick to buying groceries was to shop at the small stores and to buy dried rather than canned foods. Most of the food Vincent selected was produced in Belize, instead of the imported, factory-packaged food I had bought. If I had known earlier, I could have saved myself hundreds of dollars.

Vincent, Kurl and I drove down the Hummingbird Highway and arrived at the Cockscomb just before dark. They cooked up pigtail boil-up. I had said I'd eat whatever they did, so I dug in. It was remarkably good, but I did have a bit of trouble eating the actual pigtails. They had been salted and stewed, but still looked exactly like what they were. The rest of the boil-up was really good. The sweet potatoes, carrots, cassava, and plantain tasted great after being cooked with the pork and coconut oil. Over the next few days, I would learn how to make flour tortillas, corn tortillas, and fry jacks, all of which were excellent substitutes for bread. I also learned how to cook dried beans with pigtails and to fry plantain in coconut oil. From Vincent and Kurl's visit onwards, my grocery bills were a fraction of what they had been and the food tasted better too.

Vincent also had a whole new angle on washing dishes. Once, after I had unsuccessfully scrubbed at burnt rice on the bottom of one of my pots, Vincent put the pot on the creek bottom with rocks to hold it in place. By the next morning the fish had cleaned most of the pot out and the rest rinsed clean. Those fish were more than annoying little pests after all.

The next morning I went outside to check the weather and a brilliant green humming-bird buzzed up to me and almost hit me in the face. I found it impossible to identify the specific humming-birds, because there are about a dozen different species in the area. The bugs were bad that day, but Vincent had made a fly brush out of a piece of cohune palm. It had a solid handle and the end was bushy like a horse's tail, and worked just like one when flicked at the flies.

That morning we found jaguar tracks within 50 feet (15 m) of the cabin. I had noticed that if anyone new walked on the trails, the next day I would find fresh jaguar tracks. It seemed that the jaguars were used to me, but were curious and followed other people's tracks. Sometimes Ignacio and Pedro would bring their dog into the reserve with them, and almost always I would find jaguar tracks on the same trail the following day.

Later that day we found a partially dug-up iguana's nest in the centre of the trail. The eggs looked like ping-pong balls and I knew from previous experience that they tasted like chicken eggs when boiled. I had eaten a lot of strange foods since I had arrived in Belize. Once I ate what I thought was chicken stew and then found out that the primary ingredient was iguana. Iguanas have to come down to the ground to lay their eggs, and during the nesting season they are particularly vulnerable to predators. I had found both iguana skin and iguana egg shells in jaguar scats. This iguana nest was only partially dug up, but the few eggs that were exposed felt like they had been cooked by the sun. I covered the opening to protect the remaining eggs and we continued on the trail.

It was a good day for tracking. Later we found many tracks, including large and small ones beside each other. Farther into the grass I found several scrapes, some much smaller than others. It looked to me as if a mother had been teaching her cub the art of marking territory.

I was becoming more adept at finding and understanding tracks, and Vincent and Kurl were helping me track better. They explained in detail how they decided when the tracks were made. First it was important to watch the weather. A heavy rainfall would wash away almost all tracks, except sometimes those made in deep clay. It was raining less often now, as the dry season had just begun, but this knowledge would still be of help in determining if the tracks had been made within the last few days.

It also helped to look at the edges of the prints. The edges around older prints would crumble in time, whereas new prints had sharp edges. Often we would find only a toe print and then find nothing for hundreds of feet because of grass or other poor tracking conditions. Vincent taught me to examine the toe print carefully and try to find any other part of the print in order to determine the direction the cat was walking. When dealing with a single print it helped to measure out the approximate walking gait of a jaguar and then to crouch down and search carefully in the area the print was likely to be. At first I had been surprised at how often the jaguars seemed to be using the trails and overgrown roadways in the bush, but now it seemed logical that an animal that large would also find travel easier along a more open route. This was especially true in a place such as the Cockscomb, where the underbrush was more dense than usual because of the previous logging activities. But it was also important to remember that even though a jaguar can be as big as a person, it travels on all fours, and so is more able to travel off the trail. When tracks were faint and prints were missing, it was necessary to search the vegetation at the side of the trail for any sign of passage by a large animal. Often grass would be pushed away to form a tunnel that suggested a jaguar or other large animal had turned off the trail.

We spent most of our time on the trails, and soon I was getting better at finding and understanding tracks. It had been harder to work with Ignacio, because I saw him infrequently and often he would simply tell me where he had seen tracks and I would have to find them myself. Tracking with Vincent and Kurl was much more successful, and by the time they had to leave, I had more confidence and was now more sure that I was not walking past tracks that I just didn't recognize as prints.

Ignacio and Pedro had collected some scats for me while I was away, and they needed to be dried immediately so they wouldn't rot. I waited for a sunny day and then I dried all the scat on a sheet of zinc in the sun. Ignacio had found a scat while walking from Maya Centre that day and it was full of peccary hair. In fact so much of it was hair that I wasn't sure it was scat at first. Some of the jaguar scat looked more like balls of fur than droppings.

A few days later, we drove back to Belize City. The distance from the Cockscomb to Belize City was almost the same distance as the Cross-Country race, so Vincent said he would cycle down to visit whenever he felt like a good training ride. I said I'd feed him if he helped with the tracking. Over the next few months he cycled down several times, and I was always glad of the help as well as the company.

Two days before Christmas, I decided to spend the holiday in Belize City. I spent several days preparing for a side trip I was planning to take before returning to the Cockscomb. I was going to track jaguars in another part of the country, with the help of Vincent and his uncle Edward.

Vincent had told me about a cave in the bush where his friends frequently found jaguar tracks. The cave was near Belmopan, the capital city of Belize, about 50 miles (80 km) from Belize City. One of his friends had said that once, when he'd been out with his dog near the cave, the dog had run into it. He had heard a yelp and then found his dog dead, with jaguar tracks all around. I decided to go to the cave and set up my camera equipment and the trip mechanism inside. Vincent and I drove in to the bush area near the cave where we would stay with his uncle, who lived with his family in a small hand-built house with a thatch roof several miles past the nearest village. I had to use four-wheel drive all the way in, because of the deep mud.

Edward was a tall Creole man, about 45 years old, who had spent much of his life in the bush. His young wife was looking after two small children who were playing on the dirt floor. The walls were covered with newspaper to keep the draft from blowing through the cracks. Edward said he had put up a few articles on me and the bike race in the other room. They fed us stewed chicken and tortillas, and the two-year-old got to chew on the stewed chicken feet.

When Edward said he could use some company when he went out

hunting, I immediately responded. I don't think he had meant for me to go, but he laughed and said, "Okay, if you can ride to San Ignacio and back, I guess you can keep up!"

Though I am not an advocate of sport or trophy hunting, hunting for food is a different matter. Edward had lived off the land for years. From his few chickens he got eggs, from his milpas he got rice and corn, and from his hunting he got meat. Since he went out hunting only about once a week, and was not always successful, meat was not that common. It would have been much more destructive to the forest if he had levelled more land for cash crops and then used that money to buy meat.

I hadn't spent much time out in the bush at night and I was looking forward to it tonight. Vincent came along as well. We only had two headlights so I walked without a light. Edward walked in front of me and I tried to notice when he lifted his feet and do likewise so I wouldn't trip over anything. It was pitch-dark, and the bush was dense. I kept hitting my shins on sticks, branches, and vines because I couldn't see, but the jungle was beautiful at night. It was quiet and peaceful and I hoped that Edward wouldn't find anything to shoot. We walked for an hour and a half along logs that had fallen across rivers, through Edward's milpas, and through thick jungle. Once I reached out to grasp a thin tree for balance and gasped when I saw something coiled around it. Vincent flashed his light on it and chuckled; it was just a vine.

Normally I have a great sense of direction, but suddenly I realized I didn't know how to get back to the cabin. We had long since left the trail. Edward said that we might as well give up for the night. I recognized a huge fallen tree that we had crawled over on our way out and realized that we were almost back at the house. When we got back, I slept on a large sheet of cardboard on the dirt floor, and either it was reasonably comfortable or I was exhausted, because I was soon fast asleep.

The next morning I wanted to see if we could find any jaguar tracks. Edward had some things to do around the house, so Vincent and I went on our own. We walked along trails just wide enough for one person. Some of them were overgrown and we had to crawl through tree limbs and vines and up muddy banks. We saw a lot of tapir tracks, as well as those of paca and opossum. When the trails became too overgrown, we walked through the river.

I had brought down hiking boots and rubber boots, but had found out almost immediately that the best things to wear were running shoes. I was glad I had them on now, because they made walking in the river easier and they dried out quickly as well. Sometimes the water was as high as my rib cage and I had to hold my backpack over my head. Once I was knocked over by the current and had to really work to keep my camera from going under. We spent most of the day in the bush, and by the time we got back to the house I was starving.

After dinner Edward got out his guitar and played some Belizean folk songs. We all sang along when we could. Even the two little kids were enjoying themselves. I felt like I was part of the family. It was New Year's Eve and I couldn't think of any place I'd rather be. The children went to bed by ten, but we had decided to stay up to see in the new year. At midnight we all went outside, and each person got to shoot one bullet into the air. I shot mine last and was surprised by the gun's kick. Then we all stood outside and listened to the silence. It was a beautiful night.

The next morning the whole group of us, including the kids, went for a walk. Edward had rigged up flour bags with holes for feet and seat belts as shoulder straps, to enable us to carry the kids on our backs. We found a small hole in a rock face that Edward said looked as if it would lead to a cave. Vincent put on a headlight and barely squirmed through the narrow hole and then disappeared into the rock. Every few minutes one of us would call through the hole and he would answer back.

Then we called and got no answer. Edward was going to go in after him, but he put his head in and realized it was too small for him to crawl through. I put on Edward's headlight and squirmed through the opening. The tunnel was just barely big enough for me to crawl along the rock bottom, and within a few yards my knees were killing me. It was dark and I wondered what would be around each corner. I kept calling for Vincent, but he didn't answer. Instead of being afraid, I had no feeling at all.

I had noticed recently that whenever things happened that would have frightened me at one time, my brain just shifted into automatic. I would remain calm and do what I needed to. The change may have been the result of my having been really frightened several times here and realizing that I couldn't panic or I might do something stupid. Whatever the reason for it, it certainly was preferable to being paralyzed with fear or panicking. At least this way I could think clearly. When I got to a fork in the tunnel, I wasn't sure what to do. Just then I heard Vincent yell and Edward answer. Vincent was outside!

There was just enough room to turn around. It would have been awful to back out the whole way. I turned off the headlight and crawled toward the outside light. I had several feet to go when something shrieked above my head. I started backward into a kneeling position and something soft and living hit my forehead, then my arm, and stopped when it landed on my knee. I was relieved to discover it was just a small bat. It was clinging to my knee and making small strange noises while keeping its mouth open. It looked remarkably like it was crying. Then it was gone. I couldn't tell in the darkness if it had gone ahead of or behind me. Finally, I was outside again and Vincent was explaining that he had crawled through the tunnels until he had come out on top of the cliff. It was good to get back in the sunshine again.

That afternoon Vincent and I headed for the cave where the dog had reportedly been killed by a jaguar. We carried the motorcycle batteries to power the infra-red beam and several cameras. It was hot and we had to do a lot of walking through the river. Inside the cave we found lots of tracks – jaguar, paca and opossum.

It was a perfect place to set up the cameras: no rain and fine dry sand for tracks too. We followed the jaguar tracks from there into a bigger cave, which smelled like jaguar. We didn't have flashlights, and this cave didn't appear to have a back exit. I certainly didn't want to corner a jaguar, as the dog had probably done. We set up the cameras in a narrow passage between the large caves that was covered with jaguar tracks. I smoothed over the sand so I would know if anything walked through the beam. Large insects or bats might set it off too, and I wanted to know if I had a photo of a jaguar.

We got back to Edward's place just before dark. After dinner I went out to the outhouse and had just sat down when I felt something brush the tops of my feet. I jumped and turned on the flashlight to see a swarm of ants on my sandaled feet. A huge line of them about a foot and a half (0.5 m) wide stretched into the bush as far as my light illuminated. I stomped my feet repeatedly and most of them fell off me. Amazingly enough, none of them had bitten me. Edward came out and said they were army ants and would eat anything in their way. Luckily they didn't go toward the house.

The next morning we went out to get the camera equipment. There were jaguar tracks through the camera set-up! There were also lots of opossum and skunk tracks, and the film had advanced about eight frames. I walked through the beam myself to make sure it was still working, and the cameras clicked but no flash went off. When I picked up the flash and flicked it off and on, smoke came out of it. Now I wouldn't know if the flash had worked when the jaguar walked through until I got home. We packed everything up and took it back to the Rover. Then we drove back to Belize City.

Months later, when I finally got the film developed (there was no place in Belize to develop slide film), I was frustrated to see one skunk picture; many, many opossum pictures; and one black slide with two glowing jaguar eyes staring back at me from the darkness. The opossum had burned the flash before the jaguar had walked through.

In Belize City I met James Kamstra, a graduate student from York University in Toronto. He would be spending several months in the Cockscomb, conducting a survey of the flora and fauna of the basin. James was a friend of Joe's and had also spent some time studying tapirs in Belize several years earlier. I had spoken to him in Toronto before I left and said I would drive him to the reserve. We both picked up supplies and by the time we got to Maya Centre it was dark. The road from Maya Centre wasn't that good for driving in the daylight, but at night it was even slower-going and I was getting sleepy.

We were two-thirds of the way to Quam Bank when we saw something on the road in front of the car. It was a jaguar! It was smaller than the one Renee and I had seen, but it was still impressive. It was only in front of us for a moment, but I still remember its eyes, as it looked back at the vehicle. This one looked startled, rather than fearless, and its muscles were tensed under its smooth spotted coat. It crouched low and stared back at us with wide eyes. I stopped the car and fumbled for my camera, afraid to take my eyes away from the cat because it looked as though it would bound off any second. It paused only for a moment and then it leapt off the road and disappeared into the darkness. We both sat staring at where it had been. I couldn't believe James's luck, seeing a jaguar on his first night in the Cockscomb. That experience was worth all that night driving. I was certainly awake now.

The next day James moved into one of the abandoned cabins. We decided to hike up Ben's Bluff, since there is a trail up to it, and from the top there is a good view of the Cockscomb Basin. The trail was fairly clear, and compared to the previous week, at Edward's place, it was an easy climb, even though it was uphill. It only took us an hour to walk from Quam Bank to the top. The view was impressive. We could see most of the basin and the clearing that was Quam Bank. The basin is a broad, dish-shaped valley surrounded by ridges with the massive Cockscomb Mountains in the distance. The vegetation was different here from that down in the basin. Here it was mostly open pine forest, which reminded me of Northern Ontario. While we were looking down on the basin, a red-tail hawk flew overhead, a species that could also be seen in Ontario. It was quite close and kept flying in seemingly effortless circles. A few minutes later it flew away and a more exotic white hawk took its place, soaring above us. The bird was almost completely white except for a black band on its tail and black-tipped wings. We sat and watched it circle for a while until it too flew out of our view. Then we walked back down to Quam Bank, into the tropical broad-leaf forest.

In the Cockscomb, the dry season runs from February through April, and the heaviest rainfall occurs in August, September, October and November. It was mid-January now and there was much less rain than there had been during the first part of my study. The lack of frequent rainfall meant that tracking was becoming more difficult. I was still finding about the same number of scats, but tracks were becoming more difficult to find and were much less distinct. The clay-like mud that had been so good for finding tracks was now hard as rock. The only advantage was that the scats were not being washed away as often, so I had a better chance of collecting them now.

One day while I was drying out scat, I looked up to see a small yellow-striped house cat peering at me through the bushes. As I glanced up, it disappeared into the green. I was disappointed that it wasn't a more exotic feline. I had seen this cat several times before but never this closely. It was very skittish and had likely been abandoned here as a kitten. I had thought it was a kitten because of its size, but it hadn't grown any larger in the last few months. I wondered at its sudden appearance, so I set a piece of bacon on the ground nearby and went into the cabin. I waited a long time and then gave up and got back to work inside.

I came out later to bag the faeces, and the bacon was gone. I got another piece and was just reaching to set it down when I noticed the cat coming toward me. It saw me look up and leapt into the bushes. I left the bacon there and a few minutes later the cat ate the second piece. I didn't see the cat again for several days until I heard a mewing noise from the lawn in front of my cabin. I put out a piece of bread, but after several hours it was being eaten by ants. Obviously this cat was used to finer fare. Whenever I was alone at Quam Bank, the cat would appear around the cabin. Eventually he started sleeping just outside my screen door, on the step.

Once in a while I would feed him scraps, but often he wouldn't eat them. I didn't leave food out very often since the cat had obviously managed on his own so far and I didn't want him to come to depend on my feeding him. This cat had a very strange appetite. He loved popcorn and spaghetti and sardines. When the corn started to pop, the cat would appear, mewing at my door. After a few weeks he started bringing *me* food. After hearing a faint mew at the door, I would find small, freshly killed rodents on my doorstep. The cat obviously didn't need me for food, so I liked to think he stayed around for the company. His striped yellow coat earned the cat the name Tigger.

When I was all alone, it was nice to have Tigger as company. I had started to talk to myself once in a while, and somehow it seemed more sane to be talking to the cat. I didn't pick him up, nor did I let him in the cabin. Like the jaguars, this cat was surely carrying many parasites. One day I dropped an egg on the porous wood floor of my cabin. I was just deciding how to clean it up when I heard the cat at the door. Perfect timing. When I scooped the cat up to set him down in front of the egg, he went crazy. I don't think he had ever been picked up before. The cat was clawing at the door to get out and, when I opened it, shot off the front steps onto the grass.

I was worried that Tigger might never come back, but then I noticed he had egg on his chin. He licked off the egg and walked back to the door. This time I picked Tigger up very gently and set him down right in the egg mess. Tigger cleaned the floor better than a bucket of water could have done. From then on, I had to fight to keep Tigger out of the cabin. I'm sure he was convinced I always had eggs on the floor!

Two friends of James's came to visit, and we all went out on the back trail. A rufous-tailed jacamar flew from branch to branch on the side of the trail. Jacamars are one of my favourite birds. They look like a big humming-bird that has learned to slow down. They have the same long, slender bill, bright green backs and wings and a long tail. Farther along the trail I spotted a black-tail snake that was 4 feet (120 cm) long. James caught it, and we all took turns holding this impressive and surprisingly docile specimen. It didn't seem to mind at all.

One short stretch of trail always seemed to have new scrapes on it. I would often find fresh scrapes right beside older ones and wondered if it was the same cat, remarking the area, or a cat from an adjacent area. Since most of the scrapes along this particular stretch were made on grass, there were no tracks. I measured each scrape and noted which compass direction it was in, and the distance between it and the next nearest scrape.

One day, when I had walked past the last scrape on that stretch of trail, I looked ahead and saw what appeared at a distance to be numerous scrapes. When I got closer, I realized they weren't scrapes at all. A herd of peccaries had obviously been through the area and had been searching for food. The ground was all churned up, and tracks similar to those made by pigs were everywhere. It looked like it had been a big herd. I followed the tracks from the main trail to a small trail off into the bush. The trail was just big enough for a peccary to follow, so I decided not to crawl after them. There were several droppings that looked very fresh and I didn't want to crawl face to face with a peccary in a bush tunnel wide enough for one. It was amazing how much they had dug up. Now I understood why farmers got angry when peccaries went through their fields.

One of James's friends had brought a very powerful flashlight, and we all went out at night and shone it into the bush at the side of the trail to try to pick up eye reflections. We saw what looked like a kinkajou, a nocturnal member of the raccoon family that rarely descends from the tree-tops. But it was too high in the trees to be sure. Until then, I had only seen kinkajous in zoos. They look more like monkeys to me than raccoons, since they have round heads, short faces and a long, narrow tail they use for gripping branches. Their hair is soft and woolly and their claws are sharp. Kinkajous spend their nights searching for fruit in trees, which has earned them their local name "night walker."

One day I was driving the truck back from Maya Centre, and the roads were particularly bad since it had rained heavily the previous night. I was coming down a hill and trying to miss a log in the middle of the road when the truck suddenly swung sideways and went crashing off the road into the bush. I hadn't been going fast and I was not hurt, but I didn't understand why it had swung out like that. I had heard a lot of snapping when the truck hit the bush but it had sounded more like vines and small branches than metal. I started to open my door and realized that the truck was suspended in mid-air on vines and that my side of the truck was hanging over a low cliff. The bush had been so thick that I had not been aware that the ground dropped off like that. Several more vines snapped and I dove out the passenger door. I sank past my ankles in mud.

I was afraid that the truck would fall over the edge of the embankment any moment, but there was nothing I could do about it. The only good news was that, because I was so far off the road, there would be room for another vehicle to get by. I walked the rest of the way back to Quam Bank in the mud, carrying all the supplies I had picked up in town.

James's friend later drove me back to the truck with a small pick-up. It wasn't strong enough to pull my truck out so we ended up using a hand winch to get it back on the road. After we rescued the truck, I stood where it had been and looked down the embankment. It was far steeper than I had thought. Thank goodness for strong vines. It was unnerving to think that I could have gone over in the truck if the vines hadn't held. The seat belts didn't work, so I might not have survived the fall.

After we got the truck out, I drove another mile toward Quam Bank, and the truck suddenly just stopped going forward. We tried to tow it with the pick-up, but it was a useless effort, so we gave up and left it there.

Two days later Al, the American who had sent me the lantern, dropped by to see how I was doing and to let me know I could have the lantern as long as I needed it. He had managed to get past my truck on the way in and offered to tow it back to Quam Bank with his Land Rover. Al checked under the hood and discovered that the power-steering belt was broken. That explained why the truck had gone sideways like that. It made me feel a bit better to know it wasn't completely my fault. Al towed the truck back to Quam Bank because we couldn't turn it around on the road.

The next day Al took me to Dangriga to get a power-steering belt. We found two mechanics who came back with us and brought several belts. When we got back to the Cockscomb, the mechanics discovered a leak in the transmission that was so bad that the car wouldn't shift into gear. None of the belts they brought would fit on the truck either. We took the mechanics back to Dangriga and went back to the Cockscomb. I decided to give up trying to fix the truck for a while.

Several days later, I was out on the back trail early in the morning. I had already found two scats and was walking back toward the cabin through an overgrown section of the trail when I smelled a powerful odour. Most of the scats, especially the fresh ones, have that same odour. I couldn't find the scat, and the two that were sealed in Zip-lock bags in my pack were dry and had little smell. I had been out for several hours and it was getting too hot to stay on the trail, but I knew there was a scat in the vicinity. I followed my nose and walked off the trail into the bush edge. There was an opening in the bush that looked like a jaguar had pushed through. The grass and vine tunnel went into the darkness of the bush and there the smell was strongest.

I was just about to push forward when I realized that it might be a jaguar I smelled and not its scat. I didn't have my machete with me and the vines were too strong to walk through. If I wanted to follow the low trail it would have to be on my hands and knees. It wasn't an appealing thought. Hunters had told me that jaguars often circle around people, tracking them, and I started to feel as though something was watching me. I turned to look behind me and saw the scat just off the trail in the grass. As I picked it up with the plastic bag, I noticed it was very fresh, even warm. I kept telling myself that the warmth was probably from the sun, but I really wasn't sure.

I started back toward the cabin again and noticed some jaguar tracks on the trail, so I stopped to measure them. Some were very distinct and I was surprised I hadn't noticed them on the way out. Then I found one track on top of one of my footprints from that morning. It took me a moment to realize what that meant: a jaguar had been following me on the way out. I was excited and frightened at the same time. I kept telling myself that jaguars aren't man-eaters and that, if it was going to attack me, it had already had plenty of opportunities.

I remembered reading somewhere that tigers are more likely to attack people who are in a crouched position, so I tried to stretch myself to my full height. I stood in the centre of the trail, and kept turning around, afraid to have my back facing any direction for more than a moment.

Then I decided that I was probably overreacting. I measured a few more tracks to test my endurance and then headed back to the cabin. It was hard not to wonder what the jaguar thought of me, following his tracks and carefully taking his droppings back to my cabin in sealed plastic bags. Today the jaguar had been the one doing the tracking and, now that I was back in the cabin, it seemed rather amusing.

Vincent rode his bike into the Cockscomb later that day. It's quite a ride from Belize City, but he said he needed a long ride. When he heard about my car problems, he said his brother could probably help, so we decided to go up to Belize City the next day. Since I didn't have any transportation, I had to walk out to Maya Centre and take the bus. We left Quam Bank before dawn. I walked and Vincent rode his bike beside me until it got light. Then I told him to go ahead, because he had a long cycle back to Belize City and I would be there on the bus before him. I walked along, looking for tracks and scat. I had brought my plastic bags and measuring callipers and was hoping to find some. I walked around a corner in the road and there was Vincent, standing and looking into the bushes, holding his bike. He had just seen a jaguar ahead of him on the road. When it had seen him, it had jumped into the bush, and he was trying to locate it. I wished I hadn't sent him ahead, or I might have seen it too. He rode with me the rest of the way and we kept looking.

It had taken me longer than I had counted on to walk the 6 miles (10 km) to Maya Centre. I had just missed the bus, but luckily there would be another in two hours. Vincent started on his way, and I waited by the side of the road. Finally the bus came and I got on and relaxed. I noticed a few people staring at my belt and realized I had forgotten to take my big knife off. I waited until the bus stopped at a snack bar and then undid my belt and slid the knife and its sheath off and put it in my bag. An older gentleman who had been sitting across from me nodded and said, "That's better." It took several hours before we passed Vincent on the road.

In town, I bought a used transmission for my truck and Vincent's brother Kurl agreed to bring it down in the back of his truck. I caught the bus to go back to Dangriga, where I wanted to pick up my mail. The next bus wasn't expected for four hours, but I could usually hitch a ride at Buck's Garage. Buck would tell me with whom it was okay to hitch a ride, so it was safe enough.

A Belize telephone service pick-up truck pulled in for gas. The back was filled with a spool of telephone cable that was more than 3 feet (1 m) high. I asked one of the three men in the front if they could drop me at Maya Centre, but he said they were full. I told him I was small and could fit in the back with the cable, and he told me to hop in.

As they drove down that gravel road at 60 miles (96 km) per hour, I hugged that cable spool as hard as I could. I thought I might blow off the back. Finally we reached Maya Centre and I peeled myself off and limped out of the back of the truck. At least it was a free ride.

They laughed at me and I joined in, realizing I must have looked a sight. I was covered in dust and my eyes had been watering from the wind and streaked my face. My hair had been in a ponytail when I started, but now it was probably standing up on its own. When they asked me what I was doing at Maya Centre, I told them I was studying jaguars in the basin. The guy in the middle leaned forward and said, "You must be Melanie." I didn't recognize him, but he knew about me from the bike race. They all shook my hand and wished me luck and then headed off down the road in a cloud of dust that I was glad I wasn't in.

As I headed into Quam Bank, I saw a truck dumping sand to fill in bad sections of the road. Last time I had hitched down to the Cockscomb I had gotten a ride with a supervisor of the Public Works department. I had told him that if he ever had any leftover sand it would be great if they dumped it on the Cockscomb road. This would make driving easier, at least if I ever got my truck fixed.

I didn't think they would really do it, but when I talked to the truck driver, he said that his supervisor had told him to dump sand there. A grader came in too, and the driver said he would take me into Quam Bank. I couldn't believe my luck! I showed him the three worst spots on the road and he said he'd try to fix them. We started across a bad bridge and I could hear it cracking below us. I yelled for him to back up and told him I could walk the last 2 miles (4 km). There was no point in having a great road and no bridge. It was a nice walk in and I even found two jaguar scats. It had been a lucky, lucky day.

Quam Bank was empty, since James had left and wouldn't be back for a week. I jumped into the river and washed off all the dust. It was good to be back home again.

The next day some farm workers came in to see some equipment that the logging concession wanted to sell. They were from the farm where I had asked to borrow a horse, and they said I could come and get one the next day. With my truck out of commission, a horse could provide me with some form of transportation in case of an emergency. The foreman, Ben, kept saying that it wasn't safe to be back here without a vehicle that worked. He told me that, a few days earlier, one of their horses had been killed by a jaguar. They had lost a few cows over the last few months and had assumed they were killed by jaguars, so one of the hunters had killed a mother and her two cubs. They invited me to photograph the skull they had kept and to take measurements.

It was always difficult to tell if the cattle-killing stories were made up after someone had shot a cat. I asked if the cows might have been killed by something else and they said it was possible, but they wanted to make sure. One of the men said he had seen a jaguar grab a calf and start to carry it off. Its mother had charged the jaguar and the jaguar had just held the calf in its teeth. When the cow reached the jaguar, the jaguar slapped the cow with its paws, breaking a horn. When the cow died later, they saw that its skull was cracked. Stories of the power of the jaguar – pound for pound one of the most powerful cats in the world – made me glad that they didn't attack people.

The next day a Public Works truck came in to check the entrance road. On their way out the crew offered to take me and my saddle out to the farm to get my horse. I had always dreamed of having a horse when I was younger, but we could never afford one. For several years, before I figured this out, a horse was the only item on my Christmas list. Then I had found a riding stable where I could ride for free in the evening if I worked all day, teaching camp kids how to ride and cleaning out stalls. I had learned a lot about riding and about caring for horses during those years and was looking forward to having a horse at the Cockscomb.

It was a young horse that barely looked old enough to ride, but I was assured it had been broken in. Ben helped me adjust the tack to fit the horse, and then I swung up and we adjusted the stirrups. The horse was calm enough, so I expected no trouble. Most of the workers, including Ben, were not Belizean and many spoke only Spanish, so Ben translated comments and instructions. He led the horse to the road and let go of the reins. The horse stopped dead. I loosened the reins and kicked lightly. It turned its head and looked at me in surprise. I heard snickers from our audience.

"Has this horse ever been ridden before?" I asked. Ben grinned and said, "We use it all the time." It didn't seem possible, and then I thought of one explanation. "It's a pack horse, isn't it?" I asked. Sure enough it was used to being led with bags of plantain on its back. No wonder it was surprised when I moved.

Finally I got it to walk down the road, but it refused to cross a bridge about 650 feet (200 m) farther along. Several people had followed along behind, no doubt anticipating this event, and they proceeded to wave their arms and shout until the horse crossed the bridge. I had ridden many horses in my time, but never one that didn't understand that cues came from the rider. It walked incredibly slowly, and I began to wonder if this horse would save me any time at all.

After two hours, when I was halfway to Quam Bank, Ben and some friends showed up in a Rover to see how I was doing. I was beginning to feel like the entertainment of the week. I disappointed them a bit, and caused one to lose a bet that I would have to get off and pull the horse through the river. They could see by my dry running shoes that I had ridden across, but I didn't mention that I had had a 20-minute argument with the horse before it would cross. Ben told me if the horse gave me too much trouble they could get me a better one, and then they drove off.

We were still a mile from Quam Bank when I felt the horse shift underneath me, and just in time I realized it was about to lie down and jumped off. Probably it was as fed up with me as I was with it. I gave up and led it the rest of the way, which it enjoyed much more. By the time I had walked the rest of the way back, carried its tack up to the cabin and brought it a pail of water, I was beginning to wonder which of us was the dumb animal. After all, I was the one doing all the work. I'd have to do something about that. In the meantime I tied him in the shade of a tree near the cabin. I didn't want to find out that the stories of jaguars eating livestock were true.

The next morning I walked up to the section of trail that had all the scrapes on it. I had numbered stakes and decided to put them in the ground in the centre of each scrape, to make sure I didn't recount any. Within the first mile I had put stakes in 28 scrapes. I also found a scat on the same stretch of trail, but it was already dried by the sun. I wouldn't be able to use it for parasite analysis, just to determine food habits.

I had noticed some distinct tracks made in deep sand on the way out to the scrape site, and on the way back I decided they were good enough to make plaster casts of. All of the prints were made by one jaguar, walking in a straight line across the sand. It had been a long time since I had found several paw prints together. Since there was a line of tracks, I could measure the difference between the paw prints to determine the length of this animal's gait. By the time I had mixed and poured the plaster of Paris and waited for it to dry, the sun had burned my neck. At least it was hot enough to discourage the bugs. I cut the plaster casts out of the ground and took a large piece of sand with them. I wanted to make sure they were completely dry before I brushed the sand off.

I walked back to the cabin and set the casts sand-side up in the sun and within hours the sand was dry and hot. When I brushed off the sand, each of the three casts looked so different it surprised me. If I had found any of these paw prints on their own I would have thought they had come from different animals. The one back print was tiny compared to the front. I knew that the front feet of these cats are much bigger than the back ones, but this was a huge difference in size. One front print looked as though it was made by a medium-sized jaguar and the other front print was one of the biggest I had ever seen. It made me realize the importance of having a full set of prints before deciding on the size of the animal. The size and shape of the tracks depended so much on the type of soil and the weather conditions that it was difficult to be sure whether tracks had come from the same animal.

I had read that it is possible to tell males from females from the prints, but this hasn't been proven. It is true that the largest tracks are likely made by males, since adult males are larger than adult females. But it is almost impossible to tell if a smaller track is made by a juvenile male or a female. Some researchers have written that males' paws are a different shape from females', but no one had ever done a check on this with a large number of zoo animals or collared animals to prove it.

I would find many single jaguar prints, but rarely would I find a complete set because of the overgrown trails. Consequently, I wasn't getting a lot of information from tracks, but the scats were helping me determine what the jaguars were eating and what parasites they had.

The scats lost much of their odour when dried, but they could still be smelled through the plastic bags and the pigtail buckets I had stored them in. My cabin developed an interesting aroma, and I wondered if the jaguar tracks that I would sometimes find near the cabin were from a jaguar trying to figure out what was going on. Vincent seemed to be able to identify the prey species in the scat by looking at the hair and bones. Later I took the bones to the museum to have them identified more scientifically. I was impressed when Vincent's list matched their identifications almost exactly, even though he hadn't had a reference collection to compare samples to.

From the beginning of my study in August, until January, it was the rainy season, and during that period the most common prey item in the scat was paca. Smaller rodents, armadillos and peccary remains also frequently appeared in the scat during the rainy season. I found the remains of collared anteaters, birds, frogs and several snakes in the scat collected in the rainy season as well, but these were much less common.

In the second part of my study, from February to April, it was the dry season; at that time I noticed that scat samples no longer contained peccary hair. Peccary breed throughout the year, but more young are born during the rainy season, which might explain why they were more likely to be eaten in that season.

I also was starting to notice that I was finding even more scats with armadillo remains in them during the second part of the study. Paca and smaller rodents were not seen as often in the scat now either, but I often found scat with bird feathers in it. At this time, many birds were nesting, and several were ground-nesting species, so they were easier prey for jaguars.

The jaguars seemed to be including all sorts of strange animals in their diet. I had scats that contained snake, opossum, agouti, brocket deer, collared anteater, iguana and even skunk. I wondered what species of snake the jaguars had eaten. In a place such as the Cockscomb, where several species of poisonous snakes are common, it didn't seem smart to prey on snakes, unless jaguars had some way of differentiating the poisonous ones.

I compared my results on the jaguar's diet to the previous study Rabinowitz had made, expecting to find several differences between the two. The logging camp at Quam Bank had been in operation, and hunting was allowed in the Cockscomb during much of the period of Rabinowitz's study. The loggers often killed the jaguar's prey, such as peccary and paca. As expected, paca and peccary were jaguar prey more often during my study, when they were protected from hunters, but the increase was only slight.

Compared to the previous study I found fewer armadillos and collared anteaters, and more pacas, small rodents, birds, peccaries, snakes and turtles. The greater number of smaller prey items in my study and the fact that armadillos (which are more difficult to learn to kill) were less common, suggested that the animals in my study were younger and less-experienced hunters. Since at least six adult jaguars had been killed in the area during the time of Rabinowitz's study, and their territories might have then been occupied by younger animals, if no other adults were available, such was likely the case.

I wouldn't be able to analyze the faeces for parasites until I got home, and even then I found I needed expert advice to identify the different types of parasite eggs. Dr. Sharon Patton in Knoxville, Tennessee, had identified the parasite eggs in the samples that Rabinowitz had collected, so after I got home, I visited her lab. We identified 11 different species of parasite eggs or larvae from the faeces.

I was amazed at the number of parasites some of the jaguars were carrying. Some of the cat faeces contained six different species. Because egg production occurs in cycles, there could have been even more than six species in a cat's system at one time. One species of hookworm was found in most of the faeces, and tapeworms and roundworms were also common. Even the eggs of lung flukes, which are coughed up and then swallowed by the cats, were found in the faeces. I could study only those parasites whose eggs went through the digestive system. The jaguars probably had many other parasites that could not be detected. Some of these jaguars must have been feeling pretty poorly.

Some parasites are more likely to infect younger animals, and several of these parasite species were much more common in my study, which was further evidence that I had worked with a younger population of animals than had Rabinowitz.

It was not encouraging to find that the jaguars in my study might be young animals. That meant that, instead of the dead jaguars being replaced by surplus adults that are often common in healthy mammal populations, they were replaced by young, inexperienced jaguars, which suggested that the surplus of experienced adults had not been available. The jaguars in the Cockscomb may have been protected just in time. It was possible that even one more generation of hunting in the Cockscomb could have had long-term devastating effects.

# 7

# BRINGING IN THE JAGUAR

Although I had collected quite a large number of scats, I still wanted more jaguar-track measurements. I decided that, for the rest of my time in the Cockscomb, I would concentrate on trying to bring the jaguars into bait areas, rather than following them wherever *they* went. I would try to attract the jaguars into areas with good tracking sand, instead of waiting for them to step on the few good tracking spots that were left on the back trails. This might give me an idea of home-range areas, if I found different tracks at different sites.

I had been using catnip for my trip mechanism, but it didn't seem to be attracting any cats. I had also tried sardines since they were inexpensive and might attract margays, ocelots, jaguarundis or even foxes. I thought I had met with some success with the sardines because every time I put them out, several pictures would be taken and the sardines would be gone by the following morning. Unfortunately, when I finally did get the photographs developed, they were only wonderfully candid shots of Ignacio's dogs and of Tigger.

Hunters often use tethered pigs or cows to attract jaguars. Pigs were a lot easier for me to handle than cows, so I decided to use pigs in cages as bait. I found out from Ignacio that I would have to buy pigs from one of the other Mayan villages because Maya Centre didn't have pigs. He said his wife could go with me to help me find the village and bargain for a good price per pound.

Several cages had been left at Quam Bank after a previous study on small wild cats. After I cleaned them and made sure they were in good shape, I decided where the cages should be placed along the trail. I was still finding scrapes and scats on the trails. My horse was learning quickly and was just starting to be helpful, since it could transport things that were too heavy for me to carry around all day. Now I could bring along more camera equipment, in case anything appeared on the trail, and I could also carry more plaster of Paris and food. The machete could easily be strapped to the saddle, and that meant I could clear any parts of the trail that were overgrown.

The first day I took him out on the back trail, my horse jumped sideways on a bridge and fell through the rotten opposite side that I had been trying to avoid. His left-front hoof broke right through the bridge; he was terrified. I tugged and tried to help him out until he finally got free. Most horses would never have wanted to cross the bridge again, but my horse followed me across to the other side.

Though he wasn't very intelligent, he was a good-tempered animal and he took to me quite fast. He soon enjoyed going on the trails. It was difficult to find anything solid to tie him to when I was out on the trail because of the vines and brush surrounding most trees, but I soon realized he didn't need to be tied up. If anything he was too friendly. Several times when I was engrossed in measuring tracks, he would nudge my back with his nose. The first time he did that he startled me and I jumped. The last thing I was expecting here in the wilderness was a tap on my shoulder. Around the cabin, however, I would tie him up because he knew that the road past the cabin led to his original home.

Several times when I was walking near the cabins, I saw a gray fox. He would sit with his head cocked to one side and watch me with great interest. When I walked toward him, he would let me get only so close before he jumped up, ran back a few yards and sat and watched me some more. I told several other people that I kept seeing him, but he wouldn't appear for anyone else.

One day, when I was on my way down to the creek to wash up and was wearing my bathing suit and a towel and had thongs on my feet, a small, brilliant-green humming-bird buzzed up to some flowers on the side of the trail and I stopped to watch. I saw something move out of the corner of my eye and turned quickly to see an amused-looking fox staring intently at me. I walked toward it and it ran backward only a few feet and sat down again. I approached it slowly, to within a smaller distance, then stopped, and it repeated its actions. We covered more than 160 feet (50 m) this way, and then the fox came to a fork in the trail. I was taking the left fork down to the creek, and the fox ran a short distance along the right-hand one. I had just told it that I was sorry but I was going the other way and turned, when it ran back toward me a few steps and sat down. I think it had been enjoying the game.

I kept walking in the same direction, but with my head turned to see what it would do. As I walked through tall grass at the edge of the trail, I suddenly felt the grass move under my foot. I spun around and was shocked to see the tail of a snake slither by under my foot. It looked like a fer de lance.

I didn't know that people ran backward other than in comedy movies, but that day I backed up faster than I usually run forward. At least if I was facing it I would be able to see it coming. I stopped about 50 feet (15 m) away and tried to get my heartbeat down to somewhere near its normal rate. Then I stepped carefully and slowly back toward the brush to see if I could confirm that it really was a fer de lance. I must admit that I wasn't horribly disappointed that it was gone. I had to walk past where the snake had gone into the bush to get to the creek. I didn't have my machete or a knife on me now, so I took off my towel and got ready to throw it, as a last resort, if anything came out of the bush. After my swim I walked past the same spot again, but both the snake and the fox had completely vanished.

One morning I left the cabin at 5:45 to check the camera set-up. The air was misty and cool, and just past the first creek I startled two squirrels who kept scolding me until I was far along the trail. A few minutes later a laughing falcon landed on a tree just in front of me. It was an easy bird to identify because of its black eye-patches that reminded me of a clown mask. The camera film had advanced but I didn't see any tracks. It was likely that the mechanism was short-circuiting again, so I brought the cameras back.

It was much drier now and my trips for water were becoming much more frequent. As I walked to the creek for water, I heard a noise just to the side of the trail and saw a small hole in a mound of earth. It looked like it had been excavated recently. After getting the water, I walked quietly back to the hole. Now there were five small white eggs in it! I took the water back to the cabin and ran back with my camera. I approached even more quietly this time and was rewarded by the sight of a striped basilisk, a brownish-green lizard that was slightly more than a foot long and had a faded chequerboard pattern on its skin. The lizard dashed off into the scrub when it saw me, running upright on its hind legs like a miniature dinosaur. I sat very still and eventually it came back and sat just above the nest. It wouldn't go down to the eggs though, so I decided to leave before the eggs baked in the sunlight. A short time later I went back to check and if I hadn't marked the spot I wouldn't have been able to find the nest. The lizard had obviously buried the eggs where she had laid them.

Lizards weren't the only animals whose thoughts were on family matters. Several days earlier we had seen what looked to be a huge boa constrictor in the grass. As we looked closer, we saw two distinct colours of snake. It turned out to be two snakes entwined and they didn't seem to be aggressive. I guess they were mating, but it's hard to tell with snakes. They went their separate ways when I stepped up to have a closer look and I felt guilty for intruding.

Some birds were also nesting at this time and a pauraque nested on the trail near all the scrapes. Pauraques are mottled brown birds that look very much like whippoorwills and are about the size of a pigeon. They feed on nocturnal insects and can often be found on the dirt roads or trails at night, sitting on the ground. This habit had caused me trouble the first night I drove in, because the pauraques would not move until the vehicle was almost on top of them. I had slammed on the brakes many times before I realized that they always moved out of the way in time. Even though I knew there was a pauraque nest on the trail, sometimes I would forget it was there because it and the bird blended in with the leaves so well. On several occasions it startled me when it unexpectedly flew up from its ground nest by my feet.

One evening James and I were walking down for a swim in the creek. We rounded the corner into the clearing by the bank and I saw the most beautiful bird I had ever seen. It was almost 3 feet (90 cm) tall, with a long neck and long legs. It had a bright chestnut belly and a vivid glossy-green back and was slender with a long bill and an extremely long neck. James whispered that it was an Agami heron, a seldom-seen species that frequents streams in remote tropical areas. Less than 50 feet (15 m) away, it looked at us with surprise when we popped into view. It was standing in the shade in shallow water on the edge of a small gravel island. Suddenly and noisily it jumped into flight, and I will never forget how its bright green and chestnut feathers reflected the rays of the setting sun as it flapped away.

James had reported that he had seen a flock of scarlet macaws several miles to the west of Quam Bank, while walking on the back trail. We went out again, a few days later, but we would be lucky to find these huge red parrots again. Scarlet macaws are now extremely rare because they have been pursued relentlessly for their feathers. Parent birds are often shot and the young taken from their nests to be sold as pets. The pet trade had all but wiped out scarlet macaws, and few people saw wild flocks now.

We had just turned around to head back when I heard an incredible raucous screeching from above the trees to our left. It was the macaws. They were flying above tree-top level and I could barely make out the red colour against the sky, but there was no mistaking the macaw silhouette. They were gone as quickly as they appeared, but I felt lucky to have seen them at all.

I had heard that for every single macaw that is successfully brought into Canada or the United States illegally, more than a hundred die on the trip. Macaws, and the other species of parrots that are smuggled across borders illegally, are extremely noisy birds and must be muffled with rags or drugged to keep them quiet. Many birds die in the process, but the price of macaws is so high that it keeps the smugglers trying.

The macaws I saw in the Cockscomb looked very different from any I had seen in captivity. They were magnificent birds, squawking loudly as they flew together high above the canopy.

Trading exotic animals as pets is one of the most inhumane practices there is. I had been told of lion cubs being kept in one-bedroom apartments in Toronto until they grew too big and too dangerous. Then they are either put down or transferred from owner to owner until they die, usually from poor care. Wild animals belong in the wild, and there is no excuse for this cruel business.

I was on another trip down to the creek for water when I crouched to splash water on my face to cool myself from the midday heat. I was blinking water from my eyes when a dark furry head emerged from the creek, right beside me. I sprang to my feet in shock and stared into the sparkling eyes of an otter! Finally, I had seen an otter, or "waterdog" as the Belizeans call it. I had often found their droppings on rocks by the side of the river, but I had never seen one in the Cockscomb before. It was as surprised as I was and quickly disappeared under water.

Ignacio walked in to Quam Bank one morning and had some disconcerting news. He had met a man walking away from Quam Bank on his way in whom he recognized as someone who had been causing trouble in several nearby villages. The man had been in an insane asylum for a while, but had obviously either escaped or been released. Ignacio had tracked the man's route backward and found that he had been in Quam Bank. As I was talking to Ignacio I turned and saw that my truck had a flat tire. Maybe it was a coincidence, but it made me feel very uneasy.

I found out from Vincent later that Ignacio had said that the man had chased after a policeman with a machete in a nearby village, and then had announced that he was going to the Cockscomb to kill the white people. The man had worked for the logging camp in the Cockscomb and had been fired; he obviously didn't know that it had stopped operating a long time ago. There was nothing we could do, except keep our eyes open. The Cockscomb had always felt safe and private to me. Now I wasn't so sure.

One morning I went out to saddle my horse and he wasn't there. The rope was missing too. Ignacio came in later and said that the horse had walked out to Maya Centre, so I must not have tied him up well enough last night. I always made sure the knot was secure, so I was surprised that it had come undone. The next night, after I had gone out after the horse and ridden him back to Quam Bank from Maya Centre, I double-checked the knot.

The following morning I was standing talking to James on the steps of my cabin and the horse walked by, dragging its rope! James grabbed the rope, and I tied the horse up again. I was starting to worry that someone was untying the horse. Maybe it was the man from the insane asylum, who had been seen around the Cockscomb again. He had been dubbed "the crazy man" and I wondered if I should lock the wood door of my cabin at night.

Late one night, when James and I came back from Dangriga with some tourists, James found the crazy man sleeping on the floor in his cabin porch with a machete beside him. By this time we had all heard elaborate stories about how violent this man was. James and his friend Kirk were afraid the man might go berserk if they woke him, and the man's machete was too close to him to move it without waking him. They decided it was safer to leave him there until morning. James and Kirk locked themselves into the sleeping room of the cabin, and the next morning the man was gone. After that incident, I carried my machete more often and locked the cabin door even when I was only going out for a short time.

Several days later James and Kirk decided to spend a few days hiking up a nearby mountain. I wasn't looking forward to being alone in the Cockscomb with "the crazy man" around. My truck still wouldn't start, so James left me the keys to his jeep in case of emergency. His jeep wasn't very reliable either, so I was hoping I wouldn't have any problems. I walked down to the creek to get water shortly after they left. I was nervous enough that I took my machete with me, but doubted if I would be able to use it effectively as a weapon. When I returned, I went to check on my horse and he was gone! Now I knew that the crazy man was responsible for untying the horse, because I had made sure of the knot this time. I was angry, but I was also frightened. Suddenly I realized that the man could be watching me now, from the bush. I was trying to decide if I should lock myself in the cabin or continue looking for my horse when I heard a vehicle coming in to Quam Bank. A small group of tourists had come in to spend a few hours looking at birds in the reserve. Ignacio had sent a message that my horse was back at Maya Centre. When the tourists left, they gave me a lift out with the saddle. Half-way out we met Vincent. Was I ever glad to see him! He had cycled the 125 miles (200 km) from Belize City for exercise and planned to ride back the next morning. He wanted a place to stay for the night and couldn't have picked a better time for it.

I rode the horse back to Quam Bank and tied him up securely near the house. That night we heard a crash over at James's cabin and the next morning we saw that the rotting back steps to his cabin had fallen through. It looked as though someone had tried to break down his back door. Vincent checked all the abandoned cabins and found one that was obviously being lived in. He found some food containers that he recognized; they had obviously been stolen from James's cabin.

Vincent decided to get the police. Before he left to ride his bike the 28 miles (45 km) to Dangriga, I nailed my door so it couldn't be opened from the outside. Vincent told me if the crazy man tried to get in through the windows I was to hit his hands with the machete. Then he was gone, and I sat with my back to the wall and a machete in my hands, listening to every noise and staring out the windows.

I was beyond being scared now. The cold unfeeling had even left me and I just felt sick. I tried to imagine what I would do if he tried to get in. I couldn't imagine myself chopping at him with a machete, even if, as Vincent had said, he tried to get in through the window. So I tried to get myself psyched up. I felt completely isolated. There was no way for me to contact anyone.

Everything else that had gone wrong while I was here had been easier to handle and had worked out all right. But maybe this was too much. This man could easily kill me, and I had to remember that if he tried to climb in, I would only have the advantage for a moment. Once he was inside, I wouldn't have a chance.

I was holding on to the machete so tightly that my arm ached. After a while I started to relax slightly and then I saw a shadow at the bottom of the door. It was too soon for Vincent to be back. I called out "Who's there?" in what was supposed to be a firm voice, but got no answer. I held the machete tighter and moved toward the door. I knew I had to attack before I was attacked, but I didn't know if I could do it.

I heard scuffling noises at the door and then saw a tiny paw reach between the cracks. It was Tigger, probably trying to figure out why the door was closed. I patted the little paw through the crack, and it made me feel better. Somehow Tigger always showed up at the right time.

After what seemed like a long time Vincent came back alone. He told me the police wouldn't come. They had said that the bush at Quam Bank was too dangerous, that the man might attack them from behind, and even armed with guns they wouldn't be able to protect themselves against a machete ambush. They were obviously intimidated by the crazy man as well.

My horse was missing again, and Vincent had not passed it on the way in, so it had to be back here somewhere. It was getting late so we couldn't go out looking until morning. We searched for the horse all the next day, but there were so many places it could be that it seemed futile. Even if we were within several yards of the horse, we might not spot it in the thick bush.

The next morning we still couldn't find the horse. Vincent and I were looking together now, because it didn't seem safe for me to be alone. Vincent could use a machete better than anyone I knew, so as long as the crazy man didn't have a gun, I felt safe with Vincent. I was beginning to wonder if we should just leave Quam Bank, but I thought we had better find my horse first. We walked up some of the back trails, but since I had taken the horse on all the trails many times it was impossible to follow tracks. Three days after his disappearance, we still couldn't find the horse. I decided to drive James's jeep to Dangriga to see if the police would come in now that a horse had been stolen. We drove to Dangriga, but the police still wouldn't come in.

Ignacio met us at the Maya Centre gate on our way back into the Cockscomb and told me he had found the horse, but he had a funny look on his face. I asked him if the horse was alive and he said yes, but barely. He had found it on one of the back trails after we had left, tied in the sun for almost three days on a very short rope. He said the horse had been badly hurt and then had been left standing in the sun. Ignacio handed me some medicine for the horse and told me how to put it on the wound. I asked him if he thought the medicine would work, and he said no, but it would help until I could find a vet.

We drove in to the cabin and I saw the horse standing behind some bushes. I braced myself and walked around the bush. The horse saw me and tried to walk toward me, but he couldn't lift his head. Someone had used a machete to cut out a large section of the back of its neck. Maggots were crawling through the huge wound where his mane used to be. The wound was several inches deep and almost a foot long. Much of his mane was missing, and muscles and tendons had been cut out. It looked disgusting. I started to untie him so he wouldn't hurt his neck on the rope. Ignacio had been so upset, he had tied knot after knot on top of each other. I undid five and there were still a dozen more, so I called Vincent to bring a knife.

The horse tried to lift his head again when I called. I started to cry but kept talking to him to keep him calm. Vincent brought the knife and when he saw me crying he said angrily, "I'm going to kill him for doing this. Why couldn't he at least have killed the horse?" I tried to put medicine on the wound gently and Vincent took the bottle from me and was a lot rougher. But the horse didn't seem to feel anything. I got some water from the creek and by the time I got back Vincent had cleaned most of the maggots out.

Ignacio had said that he had found a small burnt-out fire near the horse. Vincent told me that meant the crazy man had eaten the part he had cut out of the horse and was probably keeping the horse alive so he could continue to get fresh meat. The horse looked so pathetic that I wanted to explain to it that not all people were that cruel. It moved its head slightly so that its nose touched my calf. My hands were shaking uncontrollably and I felt totally helpless. I knew I had to get a vet and have the horse put down.

I drove off to find a vet and Vincent stayed with the horse. It took me over two hours to find the vet and then he said he couldn't come until morning. It was almost dark now, so I headed back to the cabin. Vincent was making tortillas, but I told him I wasn't going to stay here tonight with that cruel man somewhere on the loose. He might set the cabin on fire or who knows what else. Vincent said, "We don't have to worry about that anymore. The guy's tied up to a pole on the other side of James's cabin."

Vincent kept cooking, so I figured he was kidding. "Sure he is, and how's the horse?" Vincent smiled and said it was fine and then asked, "Don't you want to see the guy?" When I realized he was serious, I asked him what had happened. He told me. "I went down to get some water at the creek and I saw him looking through the bushes at me, so I just kept walking until I got out of sight. Then I snuck up behind him through the bushes and surprised him. He had a machete in either hand and we had a bit of a machete fight, but he wasn't fast enough."

"Did you get hurt?" I asked, even though I could see he was fine. Then images of someone in pieces tied to a pole flashed through my head, but Vincent said he had been careful not to hurt him badly. We walked over and there he was, tied up to a post. "Please, miss," he said, in a child-like manner, "could you untie me? That man was mean to me." He nodded toward Vincent.

I knew Vincent was good with a machete, but the crazy man was about half a foot taller which is a real advantage in a machete fight. Vincent didn't have a scratch on him, but the crazy man had a cut on both wrists and one on his forehead, though neither was very serious.

I asked the man, "Why did you hurt the horse like that?" He answered, "Me hungry." Vincent got angry then and told him that he had seen his cabin and he had enough food in there to last him for a while. Vincent said we should take him to the police station, but to do that we would have to untie him. I didn't want to take any chances, so we decided to find some policemen at a nearby village.

It was getting late by this time, so Vincent had to wake up the policeman. He brought a gun along and a friend who wanted to watch the excitement. When the policeman saw how tall the crazy man was, and recognized him as the man who had previously chased him with a machete, he didn't want to untie him. Vincent untied him and then tied him back up in the back of the truck.

The policeman and his friend looked at the horse and asked if I wanted them to shoot it for me. Since it was in such pain, and looked like it couldn't possibly recover, I decided it might be the best thing. I told them I had already called on a vet to come the next morning. They said it would be better if the vet put the horse down.

We drove to Dangriga and the police there were relieved that Vincent had caught the man. They said they would call us back for a court appearance in a few weeks. We later found out that the crazy man had been killing the cows for which the jaguars were shot. I was angry until the trial, but then it was obvious that the man was mentally ill. He stayed in jail for several months.

A year later, Ignacio told me that the man was so disturbed that as soon as he was released, he severely wounded his mother with a machete. All we knew the night we brought him to the police station was what he had done to the horse, and for that alone I was glad he was out of the Cockscomb. I was relieved that the whole ordeal was over, but the fear and disgust took a long time to dissipate.

The vet arrived at Quam Bank the next morning and decided that although the horse was in bad shape, it might live. He gave me some more ointment and said to apply it and wash the wound twice a day. He said it might die anyway, but it was worth a try. The horse's owner agreed with the vet's advice. I disagreed with him, because I thought the horse was in too much pain, but I was not the owner so I agreed to keep treating the horse.

I spent an hour every morning in the creek, washing the blood and ointment off the horse and applying more ointment, and then did the same thing in the evening. It was a depressing job, because I was sure the owner would put it down once he saw it. Though I knew jaguars didn't commonly prey on livestock, I was surprised that a jaguar hadn't attacked this horse. It had a rotting wound, could barely stand up, and was tied in the area that was covered with jaguar scrapes. I was beginning to think the livestock-killing stories were exaggerated. Vincent headed back to Belize City and James came back and learned of all the excitement he had missed.

I had delayed my departure from Belize from January to the end of April because of my previous illness. It was April now, and I would soon have to leave Belize for good. I wanted to try to bait in the jaguars, using the pigs, before I left. It would be much harder to set up without the help of my horse, but I thought it would be worth trying. I bought five young weaned pigs at a nearby Mayan village for a dollar a pound. I wasn't too worried about the money, because I planned to keep them for a few weeks and by the time I was ready to sell them for that price they would have more pounds on them. I had five cages and I bought a bag of corn cobs and some cabbage from the pigs' previous owner. The pigs were running wild through the village and the surrounding bush, but the owner managed to scare a few into a wooden run. She tied a rope to one foot of each pig and we put them in the truck. When we arrived at Quam Bank they went into a large cage and we fed them plantain, which they really liked. Later, I would put four pigs each in a separate cage along the back trails and one on the road to Maya Centre.

I had found some very fine sand that would be great for tracks beside the Southern Highway. If I used the same sand around each cage, I would be able to compare directly the tracks I found at each site. I used large burlap flour sacks to collect the sand and was planning to carry it from Quam Bank into the back trails on my back. I was in luck that day, because Richard Lavigne, a Peace Corps worker, came in to visit me on his motorcycle.

Richard was an archeologist, and I had first met him in Dangriga, where he had lived for several months. Belize has an abundance of Mayan ruins and Richard was particularly interested in making an official report on one of them that had been found in the Cockscomb Basin. The Belize government had only a small staff in the Archeology department and they just couldn't keep up with the number of ruins that were reported. Even after the ruins were officially reported it would take years before they were excavated. Unfortunately, ancient ruins in Belize were constantly being ransacked, and the artifacts sold. Ancient jade pieces and pottery are often bought by foreigners who either don't realize or don't care that they are the cause of this destruction of ancient sites and loss of national historical treasures.

Richard had come to visit and to see if I could show him the ruins. Ignacio had told us where they were and that was near where I wanted to put the farthest pig. Richard said he could help me transport the sand and the cages with his motorcycle. We made a travois of two long poles that dragged behind the bike with a board in between. It was similar to the sledges used by the Plains Indians, only instead of a horse to drag it we used the motorcycle.

We spent all day carrying sand back to the sites. Several bridges had collapsed and we had to drag the motorcycle across broken and rotting beams and through creeks. I ran behind the bike, unhooking the poles when they got caught in the brush along the trail. After we got the sand out, we carried two cages and then the pig that would be in the farthest cage from Quam Bank. We found what we thought was the site of the ruin, but it was hard to tell from the mounds of dirt if we were in the right place. It looked right; the mounds were similar to ones that I had seen partially excavated in other parts of Belize. It was getting dark, so Richard had to leave. But we had accomplished a huge amount of work in one day. It would have taken me many days to do all that on foot and without help.

The next day Vincent showed up on his bicycle again and said he'd help carry the rest of the cages, but I would have to carry the pigs. He loaded me up with the first pig, putting its belly on the back of my neck so I could hold its feet in my hands to keep it in place. It was squealing loudly in my ear until it got settled, and then was amazingly relaxed. It took a long time to get out to the next sand drop along the trail and I had to stop often along the way and set the pig down. Finally we got there and set up the cage as Richard and I had done at the first site. We used stakes made from narrow tree trunks, one in the centre of each side of the cage, to secure the cage. Then we wrapped wires around the stakes and through the cage to make sure no jaguars would get the pig. We made a raised covering for the cage out of cohune palm leaves, to keep the pigs in the shade. I put a bowl of water and one of food in the cage, both of which I would have to refill every day. The pig seemed quite pleased with this set-up and was happily munching on a piece of plantain when we left to go back for the next pig.

The next pig was easier because we had done the farthest one first and I was getting more adept at carrying pigs. The third pig was not so much fun. It was more upset at the start and showed its displeasure by urinating on me. Luckily I was right near a creek, so I just walked in and rinsed off thoroughly. It calmed down after that – or maybe it was just out of ammunition. It liked me better now that I was wet, probably because I kept it cool. Finally all the pigs were snug in their cages and it was getting dark. Before I returned to the cabin, I made sure to swim in the creek to remove any residual odour.

Early the next morning I started out carrying lots of food and enough water for the first pig. The other pigs were near creeks, so that would save me some weight. My pack became lighter as I walked farther from the cabin and dropped off the food in each of the cages. I was disappointed that there were no tracks in the sand surrounding the cages, and began to wonder if we had done all this work for nothing. The good news was that all the pigs looked content and happily ate the food I had brought.

For several more days I found no tracks by the cages. I didn't want to leave the pigs out for more than a week, because they were used to roaming free and they didn't have enough room to run in the cages.

After eight days of caring for him, I washed the horse's wound one last time before I returned him to the farm. I only had a short time left in the Cockscomb and the owner wanted the horse back. I didn't know if the horse could make it that far, but I didn't have a choice. He followed me everywhere, so I just started toward Maya Centre and he followed. He walked incredibly slowly and it was upsetting to watch him labour along. It took hours to cover the 6 miles (10 km) to Maya Centre and it was really hot. I decided to leave him at Maya Centre to rest for a few hours, but there was a wedding going on and the horse looked revolting, so Ignacio said it would be better to go on. It was only about another mile.

Finally we got to the bridge that the workers had scared the horse across when I had first got him. The horse was really dragging its feet by that time and I was worried it would fall over. Then suddenly it did fall. It had managed to put its hoof through a very small hole in the bridge. It just lay there, with one foot through the hole dangling above the river. It was a main bridge on the Southern Highway and after a few minutes a truck and several cars stopped and people were trying to help me move him. Ben heard all the commotion, since we were within a few hundred yards of the farm, and came to see what was happening. He reached through another hole in the bridge and felt the horse's leg. "It's broken, but we can't shoot him on the bridge. So we'll have to try and lift him out," he said. I sat down to pat the horse's head and felt like crying. This poor little horse had been through so much already and now this, within sight of home. It seemed even crueller now that the horse hadn't been put out of its misery when it had first been hurt.

Six men lifted him, and he stood up! His leg wasn't broken after all. The men tried to push him farther onto the bridge but he wouldn't move. Then they decided it might be better to walk through the river, since it was only waist high. They tried to pull and push but again the horse wouldn't move. I told them that he had been following me all day, so maybe if they let him go he would follow me through the river. I walked straight into the water and the horse followed. We walked up the bank on the other side and Ben had a stall ready for him. The poor horse was exhausted, so I patted him goodbye and left. That was one tough little horse.

Ben drove me back to Quam Bank because I couldn't have made it back before dark on foot. On the way, he told me that one of his cows had died of a snake bite and he had dumped the carcass in an unused field. A jaguar had been eating the carcass for several days and he thought I might want to wait for it to come back. But tonight it was too late to drive in. Ben also said he had found a gourd that would work as a jaguar caller and he would make one for me tonight. He said to drop by tomorrow night before I went to see the cow carcass and he'd give it to me.

The next afternoon Vincent and I showed up at Ben's. He had the jaguar caller ready. It looked great and after a bit of practice I could make it sound the way he could. I had never heard a jaguar call so I just hoped it sounded authentic. When I asked him what it was made of, he said goat skin and horse-tail hair. Then he added quietly, "From your horse's tail." I said that was nice of him to cut off a bit of his tail for me, but I stopped in mid-sentence. Suddenly I knew what he meant. "He died, didn't he?" I asked. Ben nodded and said he was sorry. The horse had been found dead in its stall in the morning. At least it wasn't in any more pain. I held on tight to the horse-tail cord, trying to get rid of the lump in my throat.

Vincent and I drove in to the field and then walked for half a mile to get to the cow carcass. Ben had said that the jaguar came just before dusk every night. We found the carcass, but by now it was vulture material only. There was no meat left and the hide was hard as rock and shrivelled. We waited in some bushes a good distance from the carcass, but nothing had appeared long after dark.

I had brought the jaguar caller that Ben had made for me and decided to try it here. We were in a large clearing and if we sat in the centre of it we might be able to attract the jaguar to the edge, so we could see how large it was and possibly get a photograph. Neither Vincent nor I had brought a machete from the truck and we sat with our backs to each other in the middle of the field. A large flock of vultures, finished with the carcass, filled a nearby tree and watched us as they rested. I hoped that we wouldn't upset a jaguar with these calls, just attract one. We called for several minutes and then waited in silence for a response. The vultures were rustling in the tree, making it difficult to hear if anything was approaching. I asked Vincent what we should do if a jaguar did charge from the nearby bush. He replied jokingly, "I can run faster than you, so I'm not worried." We called for a while, but got no response. We decided that without a machete and without knowing how the jaguar might react to the calls, it wasn't too safe to keep calling, so we found our way back to the truck in the darkness and drove back into the Cockscomb.

Early the next morning we drove back to the field to see if there was any fresh sign of jaguar but we found none. Instead, I saw an armadillo on the trail in front of me. I stopped and took out my camera and was ready to shoot, when I realized that this animal just didn't look right. I walked over to it and flipped it over with my toe. The armadillo had obviously been flipped over and scooped out. All that was left was the shell. I found several jaguar tracks in the area. Jaguars have been known to use this method on huge sea turtles that come up on the beach to lay their eggs.

I had parked the truck by a river and had to turn it around to get back out. It got stuck in the gravel and I couldn't get it out, so Vincent tried. Suddenly the bank gave way beneath the truck, and the truck began to slide backward. The back brakes were the only ones that had ever worked on the truck, but the weight of the front end was pushing the back end into the water. When it stopped sliding for a moment, I took over the wheel. I tried to drive forward, but the wheels just churned the gravel and sand beneath them and sank in farther. The creek looked like it was less than 2 feet (60 cm) deep, but the creek bottom was soft and the truck was sinking. I was holding all my camera equipment over my head because the water was up past the bottom of the steering wheel and the truck was still sinking deeper. Finally it stopped sinking and I opened the door and carried my camera equipment over my head to the bank. The cameras were worth more than the truck, so I was relieved they were dry. Vincent and I blamed each other for a few minutes and then looked back at the truck and started to laugh. That truck had been trouble from the first day I bought it.

We headed toward the main road and met a man on a horse. He said he thought he could pull the truck out with his horse if the three of us pitched in. He was wrong. We tried for a few minutes and soon realized it was impossible. He went to get Ben who came back with a tractor and pulled the truck to the farmhouse.

As we were pulling up the driveway, Richard drove by on his motorcycle. I had planned to be gone only for two hours this morning so I hadn't fed the pigs. He offered to take me back to the Cockscomb. Vincent said he would stay and try to dry out the truck. I hopped on the back of Richard's motorcycle and we hurried into the Cockscomb. He was driving fast and I couldn't see the road ahead because of the wind so I just shut my eyes and hung on.

We were almost halfway to Quam Bank when I heard Richard yell. I looked around him and there on the road ahead of us was a cougar. It was incredibly graceful and was bounding along in front of the motorcycle. Unlike the jaguars I had seen, which all looked thick and powerful, the cougar was long, lanky and agile. It leapt into the bush in front of us and Richard pulled up the bike and turned it off. We waited a while, but we didn't hear or see anything. It was the only cougar I had ever seen in the wild. We went back to find its tracks and I was amazed how few there were on the road. It had run along the road for quite a stretch, but there were only a few, barely discernible prints. No wonder I was having trouble finding good tracks now that the ground was so dry.

I picked up food and water for the pigs at Quam Bank and Richard and I dragged the motorcycle over the bridge and headed for the first pig. Richard shut off the bike before we reached the site, so we wouldn't scare the pig. We walked around and the pig was gone. Not just the pig, but the cage, the stakes and the leaf canopy. It was as if it had never existed. At first I thought this was someone's idea of a bad joke. When I looked at the sand, I knew it wasn't a joke. There were jaguar tracks everywhere. The cage had been in a clearing at the junction of two trails and we circled outward from the spot, looking for any sign. Finally we saw a slight trail through the brush and we followed it to the cage. It was so wrapped up in vines that we couldn't see into it. We couldn't budge the cage and it was obvious that the jaguar couldn't either.

It took us several minutes to cut the cage loose from the bushes and drag it back into the clearing. The pig was dead, probably from hitting its head on the cage. I couldn't help feeling bad about that, even though I knew it was destined to be bacon almost as soon as I returned it. We slid the pig out of the cage and dragged it into the centre of the sand after I had measured and erased the old tracks.

As I was smoothing the sand over a spot where the jaguar had churned up the earth, I felt what appeared to be a rock. I was just about to toss it aside when I looked more closely and saw that it was neatly chiselled into an arrowhead. When I showed Richard he said that these arrowheads were often found in or near Mayan sites. He was pleased with the find and took it with him to give to the Archeology department.

I went back to the cabin and got the trip mechanism set up. At least if the jaguar ate the pig, I would get a photograph of it. It was already past noon, but I hoped we could get back to the Cockscomb before dark and build a stand to watch the jaguar come for its kill. The way things were going today with the truck, I'd be lucky to get back in here at all tonight. I set up the camera and we went on to feed the other pigs before I returned to Vincent and the truck. There were several people helping and they seemed to think that the truck might actually work again, but I wasn't going to count on it this week.

The next morning I went back to where the pig had been killed and there was nothing left but the camera set-up. The camera had been knocked sideways but was still on the tripod and one picture had been taken. Later, when I had the film developed, I had a single picture of a jaguar in mid-day light. The previous photograph of the jaguar eyes in the dark cave had also been taken in daytime, suggesting that the cats were not only active at night. I searched the nearby bush near where the pig had been but all I could find was two tiny bone splinters that fit in the palm of my hand. I decided to bring the other pigs in, to spare them a similar fate.

I wondered if the same jaguar would come back tonight, looking for another pig. Vincent said we could build a low platform within an hour so I set up one of the pigs in the same spot the jaguar had found its meal. I picked the nicest pig, who seemed to like people and was always eating. We jokingly called her Pollyanna and she didn't seem to mind that either.

The platform was made with three Cecropia trunks in a teepee form and the boards that made up the platform were less than 6½ feet (2 m) from the ground. It made me feel slightly safer than being on the ground. I gave Pollyanna more food, and then Vincent and I climbed onto the platform. It was only about 4 feet (120 cm) long, so when I lay down on it my feet hung over one end and my head over the other. I stared intently at Pollyanna and we didn't talk at all. Eventually I must have fallen asleep in boredom.

I woke up with Pollyanna squealing loudly and jumping backward, rattling her cage. I was just trying to figure out where I was when I saw a large shadow below and to our right. It was a jaguar! Through the darkness I could barely see the spotted pattern of its coat. This jaguar looked bigger than the last one I'd seen, but it didn't have any fat on it. It looked big and lean. I guessed it weighed between 100 and 200 pounds (45 and 90 kg) but since I didn't have any experience with weights, I couldn't be any more exact. The big cat was staring intently at Pollyanna and lowering into a crouch right in the clearing, about 3 yards (3 m) from the cage.

Pollyanna squealed again and this time when she jumped she must have hit her metal water bowl against the back of the cage. The noise startled the jaguar and it jumped underneath the platform. It had responded so quickly that even though I had been staring at it I hadn't seen it jump. One moment it had been several yards away, crouching, and then suddenly, and silently, it was under the platform. Now I knew why the jaguar was such an effective ambush predator. I had fallen asleep with my camera in my hand and now, in my nervousness, I was holding on to it so tightly that it was hurting my fingers. Since I had been leaning over the edge of the platform to see better, my face was now directly above the cat and I was within an arm's length of its tail. I hadn't noticed how loud my breathing and heartbeat were until that moment. It amazed me that it couldn't hear them as clearly as I could. Suddenly I remembered that we had left the machete on the ground. I was afraid to look at Vincent, but could tell he was also motionless.

I was so close that I could see the hair raised on the back of the jaguar's neck, and see its muscles tense under its thick spotted coat. I was afraid it would look up at us, but it was much more interested in Pollyanna. It crouched low to the ground and slunk away from the platform in a circle, which brought it to the other side of the cage. As it moved I could see that its skin looked very loose, like it hadn't eaten in a while. Even through the darkness, I could see its muscles rippling, muscles that I had never seen in any zoo animal. In the moonlight I watched it move silently into position. As it crouched, ready to pounce on the cage, I moved my camera up to get a photo.

Suddenly its eyes shifted from Pollyanna to me. Keeping its eyes fixed on me, it slowly straightened its limbs from its crouched position. It didn't look at all afraid and for a moment I wondered if it would approach. I stared back at the piercing eyes, too afraid to break the stare. Though I was afraid, I was also incredibly excited about seeing a jaguar this closely. Suddenly it turned and vanished silently into the darkness.

Vincent and I didn't speak for several moments, hoping it would reappear. "Is it gone?" I asked in a whisper. "I think so, and I doubt if it'll come back now that it's seen us," Vincent replied quietly. "Why don't we try the jaguar caller? Maybe that would bring it back," I said.

Vincent picked up the caller and then grinned. "I hope we don't say anything to upset it. You never know what we're saying when we call." Though he was kidding, there was truth in his statement. Using the caller was similar to trying to get a Doberman's attention by barking at it. I hoped we weren't sending out the call of a jaguar invading this jaguar's territory, or we could be in trouble. We tried calling for quite a while, and the sound hung eerily in the misty night air, but we heard no reply. My heart was still beating rapidly from the close encounter, but Pollyanna was back to eating again.

"Can you believe how close it was?" I asked incredulously. "It's a good thing it didn't look up!" Vincent replied. "Yeah, I thought it would hear us, we were breathing so loud! And did you see how it crouched down over there? It would have sprung on that pig, cage and everything, if it hadn't seen us just then."

We tried to be quiet, in case it or another jaguar came by, but we were too excited. Every few minutes one of us would exclaim, "Wow, can you believe we actually saw a wild jaguar so close." We waited in silence again, and then heard a branch snap suddenly in the darkness behind us. I jumped and Vincent laughed. "A bit nervous?" he asked. I hoped it wasn't the jaguar circling behind us. If it was, it didn't show itself. It was more likely some other animal that we had awakened with our exclamations.

The next morning I carried Pollyanna back to Quam Bank on my shoulders, and she didn't seem to mind at all. I had promised Ignacio I would sell him one of the pigs, and I knew he wanted it for food. I had a soft spot for Pollyanna, so I found a good home for her and the other two pigs, where they would at least be allowed to grow to full size before they were eaten. My truck had finally dried out, and surprisingly it had actually started. I drove it straight up to Belize City and left it there with a big "For Sale" sign on it. Vincent's brother Kurl lent me his truck, which was brave of him after he saw what I had done to mine, and I headed back to the Cockscomb. I loaded all my supplies into Kurl's truck and drove back to Belize City.

It was now the end of April, nine months since I first arrived in Belize to study jaguars. It was difficult to believe I'd be back in Toronto soon. In a way, I was looking forward to being back and seeing my friends and family again. But I was also very sad about leaving Belize. I would miss my new friends and my life in the Cockscomb. It seemed like I had had my share of bad luck when I considered the mugging, getting sick, the car accident, Rabinowitz's contract being postponed, cutting my fingers, the crazy man attacking my horse, the truck first almost going off the embankment, then continually breaking down and finally sinking in the river. There had been several bad moments when I wished I was back at home with nothing to worry about but essay deadlines. But for the most part I wouldn't have traded places with anyone. The excitement of the bike race, the thrill of seeing my first jaguar, the night spent on the platform with Pollyanna and the jaguar below, the friends I had made and the beauty of the Cockscomb more than made up for the hard times.

A few days later I was on a plane back to Toronto. As I was driving home along the three-lane highway toward the brightly lit city, it was hard to believe that just a short while ago, I had been sitting in a jungle, calling jaguars in. It had been a wonderful adventure.

# 8

# THE FUTURE OF THE JAGUAR

I spent the first few days back in Toronto enjoying many things that I had taken for granted before my trip to Belize. It was a novelty to flick a switch and flood the room with light, or turn a tap and have either hot or cold water. I had never been much of a cook, but now it seemed so simple, with an unlimited water supply and several instant heat sources. It was nice to have clothes without holes and stains on them and even nicer to be able to throw them in a machine when they got dirty. And the telephone was an absolute luxury.

Some of my attitudes had been changed by my experience in Belize. I didn't listen to the news as much as I had before I went south, because I knew the world could survive without me. The weather was not nearly as important to me as it had been when I was in the Cockscomb, as I now spent much more of my time indoors.

Gradually I adjusted to life back in "civilization," but I still missed living in the Cockscomb. Sometimes I would spot an animal in some bushes in the city and I would strain to see what it was. After a while I stopped checking tracks in the sand around my house, since I knew they would be those of a cat or dog or squirrel. No exotic toucans or scarlet macaws would fly overhead, and no frogs chorused at night.

One blustery day I was walking up a busy city street when swirling movement at my feet caused me to start sideways and drop my books.

For a moment I thought I had seen a snake, but it was only a line of leaves, blowing across the sidewalk. I received some strange looks as I gathered my books and walked away.

When I left the jaguar reserve, its future was still uncertain. Tourists were still rare in the Cockscomb, and funding was needed to improve the tourist facilities in the reserve. When I got back to Toronto, I hoped to hear whether the Jaguar car company was prepared to help with funding. I was optimistic about the sponsorship, but I was pleasantly surprised at their generosity when they announced their commitment. The British, American and Canadian branches of the company had come together to offer a $100,000 sponsorship. It was more than we had hoped or even asked for. It covered all the expenses the reserve would face in becoming established over the next three years.

It was important to work out an operational plan for the reserve on how best to use the funds. The First Workshop on Planning and Management of Protected Areas in Belize, a two-week conference, was held in the spring of 1987 in the Cockscomb. The conference involved people from all over Belize who had an interest in the reserve. Representatives from the Belize Tourist Board, the Belize Forestry department and many other groups and government departments met in the Cockscomb to learn how to plan and manage reserves, using the Cockscomb reserve as a prototype. The conference was headed by Alan Moore, who had designed parks throughout Latin America.

I flew to Belize with Steven Price of WWF (Canada) to join the workshop. Some participants stayed in the cabins at Quam Bank and the rest were put up in Hopkins Village, several miles from Maya Centre. It was strange to be back in the Cockscomb with so many other people around. It had been almost a year since I had left and jaguar tracks were still found frequently on the trails. During our stay we even found a fresh jaguar print on one of the trails behind the cabin area.

It was decided during the workshop that Quam Bank would be used to house tourists and researchers. Trails that were in the immediate vicinity would be used extensively. Keeping tourists near Quam Bank would decrease any chance of wildlife being disturbed.

Ideally, it might have been better for the wildlife if no people were allowed into the Cockscomb Basin at all, but such a plan was not economically feasible. Instead, we wanted to show the government that nature tourism was much less destructive and generated more income than did logging or other land uses. If the Cockscomb could generate more money through tourism than it could from logging, then it would set an example for other wild areas throughout the tropics.

The income generated from park entrance fees could be used for day-to-day maintenance. Tourists coming to visit the jaguar reserve would spend money on the airfare, car rentals, gasoline, taxis, groceries, restaurants, hotels and general supplies and the benefits of this income would be felt throughout the country. Tourists would likely visit the quays just off the mainland and spend money on boats, and scuba diving and snorkelling. All in all, tourism would have far greater benefits for the whole country than would a group of foreign loggers, living in an isolated logging camp and then returning home once the area was stripped.

By setting aside the small area around Quam Bank extensively for tourism, it could be ensured that wildlife in other parts of the basin would remain undisturbed. Though nature tourism is often seen as undestructive, simply the presence of humans in an area does have an effect on wildlife. Some species, including many birds, are relatively unaffected, whereas larger mammals, such as jaguars, ocelots and tapirs, would likely avoid an area that was frequently used by humans. These animals could still be seen on the trails, but not as frequently as they might be seen in more remote areas of the reserve where tourism was not encouraged.

By the end of the workshop, the group had produced a two-year operational plan for the reserve. The plan described in detail exactly what the group felt needed to be done in the reserve. It included specific goals such as renovating buildings and creating and maintaining wilderness trails. Plans were also in the works to hire a full-time director for the reserve.

After the workshop was over, we all attended a gathering held at the Fort George Hotel. Dean Lindo, the Minister of Natural Resources, was there to show his support for the reserve, as were other government officials and agency representatives. The workshop had melted away differences between many groups through discussions and logical planning. There was no doubt it had been successful. The next test would be to see if the plans would be carried out.

Several weeks later I was on my way back to Belize again with a reporter and photographer from Britain, Jeremy Hart and Peter Robinson. They were interested in reporting on the reserve that the Jaguar car company had sponsored. I borrowed Kurl's truck again, and we headed back down to the Cockscomb.

We spent a hectic few days in the reserve, getting lots of photographs and talking to everyone involved. People were extremely helpful and we hoped Jeremy could develop a lot of tourist interest in both Canada and Britain. If the reserve could generate tourism for all of Belize, the government would not only encourage it, but might be willing to set up other natural areas throughout the wilderness of Belize.

Within a few days we were back in Toronto and Jeremy was writing frantically for the Canadian press before he returned to publish in Britain. Within a short time he had published articles in several Canadian newspapers and magazines and in many British publications. He even had an article in an Australian magazine.

Enough interest was being generated to have an impact in Belize. Within days of Jeremy's articles appearing in the Canadian press, I received several telephone calls from people planning to visit the reserve on their travels. Jeremy and others were creating a new interest in Belize that was causing an immediate increase in tourism and, therefore, tourist income, in Belize. The number of tourists visiting the Cockscomb rose dramatically as travellers learned of the world's only reserve established to protect jaguars.

Eight months passed before I returned to Belize again. His Royal Highness, Prince Philip, in his role as international president of WWF, was planning to come to Belize to visit the jaguar reserve. John Mackie, President of Jaguar Canada, and I were invited to attend a private dinner in February 1988, which Prince Philip and the governor general of Belize, Dame Minita Gordon, would attend to discuss the reserve.

I arrived in Belize a day early to make hotel and car arrangements and to make sure everything went smoothly. The following day I went to the airport to pick up John Mackie, but I was told that some of the flights had been rescheduled to accommodate the Prince's visit. I waited for several flights and when John Mackie didn't get off the last one I started to worry. Hours later there was still no sign of him. I decided to leave the airport.

I also had trouble finding out where the dinner was being held because it was so private that even the governor general's office didn't know about it. Finally I phoned a friend of mine who lived across from Government House, a government building that the governor general often used for such meetings. My friend said there was a commotion going on over there, so I thought that was likely where everyone was. I jumped into a taxi and was soon trying to talk my way into Government House.

There was a crowd of people at the gate, waiting to see the Prince. I tried to explain to the security guard that I was supposed to be inside, but he wasn't convinced. Finally I said it would be his problem if Prince Philip and the governor general found out later that one of their guests was stopped at the gate. He thought about it for a moment and suddenly swung the gate open and I was inside.

I walked up the front steps and heard a commotion behind me. I turned to see Prince Philip walking up the steps! This was obviously a very official-looking receiving line, so I scooted in through a side door and found myself in the kitchen. There I waited, standing on tip-toes, peeking through a window. Every few minutes I had to give up my spot for the cook and waitresses who wanted a peek too. Finally it was all clear and I stepped out of the kitchen, wondering what to do. I hadn't exactly made a graceful entrance so far, but I had met some fun people in the kitchen.

Luckily for me, I ran into Dr. Peter Kramer, the Conservation Director of WWF International in the hall. I explained to him what had happened and then heard a voice from behind me. "Hello, who have we here?" It was Prince Philip and he seemed quite affable, so I explained to him about the problems at the airport. The Prince was very understanding. We arranged for John Mackie and me to attend dinner on the following evening, if he had showed up by then.

A few minutes later the three of us sat down for dinner with Dr. Curt Freese, a representative of the American branch of WWF, Prince Philip's security officer and another personal assistant, and the governor general of Belize. Prince Philip rearranged the seating so I could sit beside him and talk about the reserve. I was so exhausted from running around trying to locate John Mackie that I wasn't even nervous. Peter Kramer and Curt Freese had been travelling with Prince Philip visiting WWF reserves throughout Latin America. They had just been to the Galapagos and Costa Rica and were on their way to a butterfly reserve in Mexico.

It was impressive to hear that many reserves were being set up throughout Central and South America, but it was also shocking how much of the tropical forest was being demolished every day. Every year more than 20 million acres (8 million ha) of tropical forest are logged or transformed into permanently cleared land. That is about 1 percent of the remaining tropical forest being lost every year. We talked about the jaguar reserve and how I had decided to ask the Jaguar Car Company to support it. All my dinner companions would be travelling to the reserve the next day, so I told them to keep a sharp eye out for tracks. Prince Philip is an avid naturalist and was looking forward to the trip.

After dinner I headed back to my hotel. There was still no word from John Mackie. Finally the next morning he arrived on a plane from El Salvador. The plane he had taken from Miami had been unable to land because Prince Philip's plane had arrived in Belize at the same time. There were only a handful of other people flying to Belize, so the plane had flown on to El Salvador and they all had to spend the night there. I was glad he was finally in Belize, and impressed that he was such a good sport about the whole incident. Belize is impressive enough, but it is even more impressive after spending a night in El Salvador. That night we both had dinner with Prince Philip and Manuel Esquivel, the prime minister of Belize, as well as several other government officials.

The following morning, John Mackie and I flew down to Dangriga. I had arranged for Kurl to meet us there with his truck, and he drove us to the Cockscomb. Maya Centre hadn't changed much. It was good to see Ignacio and Pedro again. Pedro's 14-year-old wife was expecting a baby any moment from the looks of it and they were both living in Maya Centre now. In Quam Bank we talked with Dan Taylor, the U.S. Peace Corps volunteer who had been helping direct the reserve, and Ernesto Saqui, who had just accepted the position as the new director for the reserve. Ernesto Saqui was well qualified for the appointment. Like most Mayans, he had grown up learning about the bush and its wildlife. He was a teacher and was Maya Centre's village council chairman, a much-respected position.

Quam Bank looked much better than it had when I lived there. It had been eight months since I had last visited the area, and I was impressed with the improvements. One of the cabins had been cleaned up and would soon be used as a visitor centre. Several acquisitions made life at Quam Bank easier. There was now a two-way radio that could be used for emergencies and to arrange visits to the reserve. The wardens and the director had a truck to take them back and forth between Maya Centre and Quam Bank. This would save several hours a day. The truck was also used to travel to local schools and villages where the preserve's personnel would explain why hunting should no longer be practised in the reserve, and why jaguars and other endangered animals should not be hunted.

This was only one part of the plan to educate young people in Belize about local conservation. Schoolbuses full of children from Belize frequently arrived at the reserve to learn more about the natural wealth of their country. A newly acquired projector was used for talks on conservation for the school children. Ignacio showed them tracks and pointed out the different wildlife as they walked the trails. He explained that the bush was not to be feared, but to be respected and enjoyed.

There had been more visitors to the reserve in that month than there had been during the duration of my stay in the Cockscomb. New nature trails had been created in an interconnecting cloverleaf pattern around Quam Bank so that there would be trails of the greatest length with the least impact on the wildlife. Signs and maps were available for visitors to plan their hikes, and garbage and washroom facilities had been set up. A camping area had been cleared, and outhouses, picnic tables and shelters had been constructed so that visitors could spend the night in the reserve. Fruit trees had been planted along the trails and near the cabins to attract birds. The main road into the reserve had received much-needed repairs.

Though many of the improvements might seem trivial, they were all important in making the reserve a good tourist location as well as a special place for Belizeans to see. Quam Bank was now a beehive of activity, but, because of good planning, almost all of the tourist activity took place in a small fraction of the reserve. Because there was no hunting allowed and because more people were in the reserve area, animals were being seen more often than before. That year peccary, margay, cougar, red brocket deer, tayra, tamandua and paca had all been sighted on the reserve. Fourteen jaguar sightings were made in the reserve in a nine-month period.

John Mackie and I were both impressed with the tremendous amount of organization and physical labour that had gone into making the workshop's plans a reality. We would later find out that the total of visitors for that year was up to 2,000, 30 percent higher than the total for the year before, which had itself been a record year. Most of the visitors were tourists from other countries and would be spreading the word on conservation.

Besides Prince Philip and John Mackie, the prime minister of Belize and his family, the Belize ministers of Agriculture, Forestry and Fisheries and Social Services, all had visited the reserve. Other visitors included 70 first-year teachers from Belize's teachers' college, and 40 students from the Belize Rural Athletic Association. Even a group of students from the University of Edinburgh in Scotland came to see the reserve.

Publicity for Project Jaguar was growing, and it became the first project of WWF Canada's "Guardian of the Rainforest" program. This public fund-raising program protects acres of tropical forest throughout Mexico and Central America. To date, more than one million dollars have been raised, and money continues to pour in. Today there are other tropical reserves receiving protection under the Guardian program. Several of these reserves are in Mexico: the Sian Ka'an Reserve, six monarch butterfly reserves, and the Sierra de Manantlan Biosphere Reserve. The program also provides funds for the Monteverde Nature Reserve in Costa Rica and the Quetzal Cloud Forest Reserve in Guatemala. The resplendent quetzal is an exotic-looking emerald-and-ruby-coloured bird that lives only in the cloud forests of Latin America. As part of the program, each person who donates $100 or more receives a print of a jaguar, taken from the painting that was commissioned by Jaguar Canada Inc., and painted by Canadian artist Rob Tuckerman.

The problems of wildlife and wildland destruction are not unique to

Belize, but are being faced by almost every country in the world. Many species of plants and animals, some of which have not even been discovered yet, are becoming extinct. Throughout the world, scientists have identified and named only about 1.4 million species of the estimated 30 million or more species that may now exist. Identification has been difficult because many species of plants and animals only exist in extremely limited habitat areas. Until recently these areas were largely inaccessible, but they are now being irresponsibly destroyed without prior scientific investigation so that we understand the implications of their loss.

The problem of extinction is particularly severe in the tropics. Tropical forests cover less than 15 percent of the world's land surface, but they hold about half of the world's species of plants and animals. Tropical areas not only have a greater variety of species, but also have many species that are indigenous to one specific location. Most samples of 2-acre (1-ha) plots of rain forest contain 50 to 150 different tree species, whereas temperate forests hold only up to 10 species per acre. The island of Madagascar, off the east coast of Africa, has more than 10,000 different plant species, of which 8,000 are found nowhere else in the world. Twenty percent of all the world's 8,700 bird species are found in Amazonia. It is difficult to determine how many and how quickly species will become extinct, but extinction rates for the next few decades have been estimated at a thousand times greater than the natural rate.

There are countless arguments for protecting rain forests. Regardless of the potential benefits to people, I think we simply have no right to destroy these last vestiges of beautifully complex ecosystems. The World Charter for Nature states it best: "Every form of life is unique, warranting respect regardless of its worth to man. . . ." The interrelationship of the earth's living things is like a precarious house of cards. The elimination of a few parts can lead to the ultimate destruction of the whole.

For those who need further arguments based on direct worth to people, there are many. Countless drugs that are now commonplace were developed from plants and animals that may not exist for future generations. There are undoubtedly many as-yet-undiscovered sources of valuable substances that may be forever lost if the destruction of wildlands continues.

Medical texts are brimming with examples of medicinal compounds originally derived from plant and animal products. Antibiotics, one of the few groups of compounds capable of eradicating bacterial and fungal diseases once responsible for epidemic losses of people and livestock, are originally produced by moulds and bacteria. It is impossible to determine how many so-far-unknown antibiotic-producing organisms may exist in rapidly diminishing habitats around the world. Tubocurarine chloride is a common muscle relaxant used in surgery. It is derived from the plant-based curare, a substance that was originated and used by South American Indians to make poison-tip blowpipe darts for hunting. Digitalis and digitoxin, two important cardiac stimulants that have saved countless lives, are extracted from common foxglove and Grecian foxglove leaves, respectively. Dried leaves must be used to prepare every dose because there is no known way of synthesizing these two glycosides. The American Indians used willow bark as a painkiller and to reduce fever. The purification of the willow's active ingredient led to the development of aspirin. Extracts from the rosy periwinkle, a small plant from Madagascar, are now being used along with other treatments to increase complete remission of childhood leukemia from the previous rate of 20 percent to 80 percent. A steroid from a Mexican yam contributed to the development of "the Pill." Maybe it was nature's attempt at protecting herself from the ever-growing population of earth! Shark liver contains lipids that increase human resistance to cancer; didemnin from sea squirts works against many viruses including colds, herpes and meningitis. The list goes on and on. If the wildlands of the world can be saved, so can this diversity of life that will benefit all of us.

The importance in preserving this diversity can also be seen in its benefits to food crops. Many crops consist of plants that have been bred to be almost genetic clones of each other. Therefore a single virus can wipe out entire crops. In the 1960s, 30 percent of Montana's wheat crop was lost because of stripe rust each year. Genetic input from a wild wheat from Turkey made the wheat resistant to stripe rust. The wild-wheat strain from Turkey was also resistant to more than 40 other wheat diseases and is said to be worth over $50 million each year in the United States. The disease resistance of domesticated corn crops has been vastly improved by the discovery in Mexico of the last stands of ancestral corn in the world. The entire species occupied an area of only 10 acres (4 ha)! Many other wild plants have been used to make crops resistant to disease and environmental conditions.

Products from the wild are still being used by industry as well. Even with the introduction of many synthetic products, rubber is still an important crop, and Brazilian rubber grows best in natural rain forests, not plantations. Natural starches, fats and oils are used in everything from cosmetics to medicines and food. Logging is still a big industry, but companies must turn to methods that provide a self-sustaining yield. Otherwise the industry has as bleak a future as the forest.

The underlying problem of the destruction of wildlands and species seems to be overpopulation in developing countries and over-consumption in developed ones. I am often asked if I think it is right to set an area of land aside and forbid people who might be hungry or homeless to live or hunt there. I don't think it is right, but it is necessary. In the long run, it increases benefits to all living things, including people. The human population keeps expanding and will probably do so until it reaches some sort of limit. The limit will be reached whether or not there are wild areas set aside, but it will be reached sooner if there are.

It is impossible to protect the jaguar, or any other living creature without protecting its habitat. The jaguar needs an area large enough to support a consistent prey population in order to survive. In turn, prey populations need predators to prevent them from undergoing population explosions that ultimately result in death from mass starvation or disease. By protecting the habitat in the Cockscomb, the jaguar, as well as the rest of the wildlife, will be protected.

When I first told people I would ride in a bicycle race to help protect jaguars, they thought I was crazy. That race had an impact on conservation, albeit a small one. Other projects may also start out small and grow. I received a letter from a young boy in British Columbia who calls himself "Marc the Jaguar." He has started a jaguar club, where he and his friends learn about jaguars and try and think up ways to help protect them. Who knows where that will lead? If more people were like Marc, and took the initiative to make a difference, more wildlands would be protected for future generations of both wildlife and people.

The Cockscomb Basin is only a small piece in the tropical puzzle, but a piece that, once lost, can never be replaced. It has been worth saving, as are all the pieces. Some areas may be set aside to be protected completely. Some may allow selective logging only. Others may allow seasonal hunting. But no wild areas should be used beyond their sustainable yield.

The future is looking much brighter now that people realize that it is not only their responsibility, but also their privilege to protect the wildlands and wildlife of the earth. For now, it seems that Belize's magnificent spotted cat has reclaimed its throne.